From my childhood, a variety of events and activities seemed to prepare me for the later surprising and potentially dangerous situations I found myself in. I also experienced the effects on different people in Apartheid South Africa and had to manage them. This led to various positions back in England that also had their moments. Developing an assessment course in management when I was a lecturer, even then and later, more surprising events followed me!

Norman Webber

INTO AFRICA – THE ADVENTURES OF A NOBODY

AUSTIN MACAULEY PUBLISHERS®

LONDON • CAMBRIDGE • NEW YORK • SHARJAH

A CIP catalogue record for this title is available from the British Library.

ISBN 9781035827367 (Paperback)
ISBN 9781035827374 (ePub e-book)

www.austinmacauley.com

First Published 2024
Austin Macauley Publishers Ltd®
1 Canada Square
Canary Wharf
London
E14 5AA

My story is primarily based on incidents between 1965 and 1970, largely of my life working at President Steyn Gold Mines, Welkom, South Africa, where I was introduced to Apartheid among other things. However, it starts with unlikely instances that I experienced from the age of two, all of which made me the person I developed into from the time I returned to the UK, again with the often unexpected to surprise me from time to time.

Having supposedly finished my story, I realised that my early life had prepared me for much that was to follow, so I have added a number of events that then seemed unimportant at the time but which shaped my character in a way that I initially did not realise.

Certainly, I had three summers until I was four to endure pneumonia and the twice-daily penicillin injections from my doctor, who managed to get the medication from a hospital in Maidstone. The only benefit was being given a sweet each time made by him when sweets were otherwise rationed.

My mum, who was born in South Africa a few years after the start of the century, was wonderful except that she always had a thing about black people that I never understood. However, she always supported what I did and encouraged me to go out on my own to walk or cycle, sometimes for miles. This definitely gave me a lot of confidence.

Something else that was important was playing draughts with my dad and later chess and variations of whist with friends or at school. I also just managed to get into the school chess team, and I managed to win most games. These taught me something about seeing problems and finding ways to win.

A bit younger when I was just eight, *The Dambusters* film led me to buy some bangers, building a dam to hold back water in the untarmacked road outside our house and putting them in it, to light and then blow the dam up several times.

Much later in life, while planning a school visit to the Ruhr, I went inside the Mohne dam that was destroyed and walked across the Sorpe Dam, which was also attacked. Those memories reminded me of my versions.

Nine years on, I knew from about October of my final year of A Levels that I was unlikely to gain good enough grades to go on to university and also that my scope for future employment was going to be extremely limited, judging by the very sparse offerings suggested by our careers master at Maidstone Grammar School.

This was largely due to the electrical rig that my dad had set up in my bedroom just after my birthday in February earlier. It consisted of flex, connected to the light socket in the middle of the room, which was somehow held on the ceiling to the right of my bed and falling to the adjacent record player on the floor beside me, to allow me to listen to the Beatles whenever I wanted.

Unfortunately, one morning, I got up a little late for my journey to school and forgot about the wire hanging down beside the top of my bed. Suddenly, seeing some form of impending doom in the semi-dark, I jerked my head violently to avoid a mishap but only succeeded in slipping a disc in my neck.

With my hand holding together an emergency collar made from rolled-up newspaper, my dad drove me to our doctor's six miles away. His only solution was lots of bed rest, flat on my back. This was sustained for about two months and until the summer term started. Even then I was banned from taking part in any active sport.

A big chunk of my A Level maths and geography curricula had been completely lost. This was made even worse by a twice-weekly visit to the hospital for physiotherapy on Tuesday and Thursday afternoons.

The memory of one of these sessions has been repeated in my mind at regular intervals in my life.

One day, I had been told by the physiotherapist to sit on a wooden chair, above which was a pulley with a brown rope, with a hook on the end, hanging down. Then he attached a leather collar under my chin and around to the back of my head, with straps leading up to the rope. After this, I was hoisted up from the chair still in the seated position.

The physio had pulled the rope down to hoist me by this hold and then stood holding the rope with a straight arm down behind his back.

There was a knock on the door, and a colleague came in. The physio turned around to look at him, and they started to talk about antiques. I lost interest at this point, as the collar under my chin had slipped a bit and was beginning to choke me. I was unable to speak let alone breathe, and I couldn't think what to do, but fortunately, the stranger intervened with alarm in his voice.

"I think you should let your patient down, his face is beginning to turn red."

I was quickly let down: sitting again with a bump, and heard the colleague leave the room while my physio apologised profusely to me.

Anyway, by then, I had no idea how I might catch up with the most difficult sections of the courses, but I did have good map reading skills gained from my time in the school cadet force and from planning where to take long cycle rides around where I lived in Kent, plus the trigonometry I had was sufficient for a career as a surveyor.

I'm not quite sure how mining surveying later came into my mind. I certainly didn't live in a mining area, but I did hanker after going to South Africa, as my mum was born there, and there were relatives living there who sent gifts of dried fruit for us at Christmas. I was also the only one in my family not to have been to the country.

My mum and older brother and sister had lived near Cape Town for a few years to avoid bombing during the war, and my dad had been lucky enough to have been posted to the nearby port of Simonstown after his ship had been torpedoed in the North Atlantic and from which he had had a lucky escape, being rescued before the cold water got him.

I'm not at all sure why I contacted the Anglo-American Corporation, it might have been because I had been told that my cousin was Harry Oppenheimer's personal private secretary, but I didn't use that connection in the application letter that I sent in November 1964.

I was a little surprised when, a couple of weeks later, a letter came from De Beers, not AAC, inviting me to an interview at their offices in Holborn, London. Of course, I accepted and arranged a time and date.

When I arrived in London, I was wearing a suit, and as I was walking towards their office, two pigeons passed over my head depositing droppings on both shoulders as they did so. A lucky omen for the interview I hoped.

The gist of it went like this: "I see you are enquiring about working as an underground surveyor in a gold mine. Well, I can offer you a job now as a diamond cutter if you like."

I turned that down, and at that, my interviewer seemed most disappointed.

"Well, if you're certain you want to be a surveyor, I'm sure we can arrange it, but you'll have to satisfy us and yourself that you can work underground first. We'll arrange it for you, and if everything goes well, we'll pay for your travel and training to get the surveying qualification when you get there." (However, that was the only promise not kept.)

I was delighted. It felt as if I floated home, rather than rattled back by train. I was also pleased because I was able to tell my dad of my future plans before he died suddenly, not long after my birthday.

My mum had gone up to bed early, in part because my dad was not well and had been sleeping badly, so she had stayed in their double bed while Dad often used my sister's old bedroom because of the pain he still suffered from after major surgery in St Bartholomew's Hospital in London, where my mum and I visited him every weekend for about a month before he could return home.

He showed us his incision that went halfway around his body when his vein and artery to his liver had been changed over.

One evening, Dad stayed downstairs with me to watch a little early evening TV. I noticed that he wasn't really watching the programme and was not too surprised when he suddenly but quietly turned and told me he was going to bed because he felt tired.

The sound of his voice and the way he looked at me seemed very odd, but I dismissed these feelings as I knew he was not well.

It must have been about half an hour later when I heard a muffled cry from my sister's old bedroom.

So I rushed upstairs, only to see him flat on his back on my sister's former bed, lips turning blue and face going a grey-white, with no sign of his breathing.

I called to my mum, tore back the bedding and immediately began what I hoped was the right technique of heart pumping, as I just guessed that it might help. But, as I pushed down on his chest, all of him seemed to disappear into the mattress, not just his chest going in and out.

I felt a failure but didn't know what to do. But I did know that a GP, not ours, lived just up the road, so I suggested to Mum that I ran up the road to try to get him, while she just stood and looked down on Dad, not appearing to realise what was happening. She stood silent, and it took a while for Mum to agree, but when she did I rushed out of the house and up the road, all the while thinking that I knew full well that Dad did not want to go back to the hospital again after the two, fairly recent, major operations from which he still had pain.

Anyway, when at last the GP sleepily emerged from his front door and said that he couldn't come, I turned and ran back towards our house. Fortunately, I could see that our own

GP had arrived by then but had no hope of resuscitating Dad. Silently, Mum and I were pleased but didn't say so.

The doctor I had tried to call came around to apologise the next morning. He understood why I had called and felt bad about not coming. But we reassured him that it would have been a waste of time anyway and that he could not have helped.

During the following days, I felt I had to be strong for my mum and sister, who had come back home to support Mum, and tried not to show any emotion but attempted to manage Dad's tasks despite wanting to cry sometimes when memories of good times with him came into my mind.

Not all of my memories were necessarily good the whole time; pictures of some of the earlier ones were the first in my mind.

The first I can recall was being pushed home by my then thirteen-year-old sister in a pram and suddenly sitting up as much as I could to see us passing a shooting break, flames seemingly all over it, with the white-painted inn behind on the opposite corner to our road.

At my age, I had no idea of its potential danger.

The following year, when I was just three, Dad had taken all of us to Margate to see the sea for the first time, as most of the rest of Kent's sandy shores were still off-limits because of war debris. Anyway, I recalled a most appalling scene from our journey.

I was sitting behind my dad in his old, black Ford known as Bess, and as we turned a sharp left-hand corner, a motorcyclist and pillion passenger coming in the opposite direction failed to turn right and shot past and straight through an opening into an orchard. Unfortunately, for them, a wire was strung across the gateway at their neck heights, apparently decapitating both of them as they sped in.

Dad didn't stop or speak about it afterwards, and as far as I was aware, we were the only two who could have seen it, so no one else ever mentioned it, and I have never been entirely sure that my memory was reliable, but the final image remains very clear; perhaps because it seemed so awful at the time. But, at that age, I don't think I had the words, and it did seem somehow unreal.

A less dreadful event happened as later that afternoon as we sat on the shingle in the sunshine, but it is one I always remember when I see my brother now because I threw a pebble into the sea that hit him on the top of his forehead and he swam. He still bears the scar today.

Otherwise, we occasionally visited Dad's mum who lived in Wood Green, London. I can still see and wonder at the thought of passing under the Thames through the brightly lit, yellow-tiled Blackwall Tunnel, then passing bomb-damaged and burnt-out buildings, or rather largely the remains of walls, en route to Gran.

Then in the sitting room playing, the only way my brother and I could, on Gran's black upright piano; me playing, or rather hitting, the high notes with one finger, pretending to be in a fighter plane firing, while my brother banged on the low notes simulating bombers bombing in the blitz.

I saw very little of my yellow-haired gran, but I always remember stopping in Maidstone on the way back to Headcorn to buy fish and chips to eat at home—a real treat then.

Most of my other memories are to do with Dad's work.

I don't know why Dad decided to take me with him during the storms of 1951, nor what work he was doing down in the Kent marshes, but what I do recall was entering New Romney and turning onto a road, fairly near to the coast, that led to Hythe and seemed to run roughly parallel to the shore.

Unfortunately, the wind was blowing strongly and bouncing the car from side to side on the raised fairly narrow road. At my height, sitting in the front seat, I could just about see outside. The storm clouds were easy, but soon I was aware of the spray that was coming from our right and, lifting myself up as much as I could, to see better what was happening. I could only see the sea, miles it appeared from where it should have been, and also completely blocking the road in front of us although the road seemed to have been raised high enough from the surrounding land to normally avoid this. But then I did not know that the weather was most unusual, and much of East Anglia had also been flooded.

Dad decided to turn back. A sensible idea I thought, as the waves were getting very close on three sides.

This was a slow, buffeted enterprise that seemed to last forever, as he manoeuvred the car backwards and forwards (no power steering then) until we were finally around and could escape. I remember how frightened I felt as he was doing this as I thought the car could be blown over into the water at any time. And what would we do then?

Mrs Collinson, who lived on the corner of our road opposite the white inn, invited me and Mum to watch the coronation of our Queen on television. It seemed incredible to me, even though it was in black and white and on a small curved screen.

I don't think there were many people locally who had the service then.

I was given quite a lot of freedom to roam when I was quite young.

The first of my adventures did not take me very far. Just down our unmetalled road to where trees overhung it, with a green-painted garage set a few feet back from the roadway. These travels occurred on darkening evenings and always there was an unknown little noise from somewhere that I could not see. It scared me, and I ran back for comfort from my mum, but really I somehow enjoyed daring the spirits to leap out on me.

The other thing that I and my neighbouring friends enjoyed doing was doing a cakewalk—a grand sort of term for a very narrow walkway above a roadside ditch where no one was allowed to grab the fence or tree next to it to stop falling into the water.

Later in life, I repeated the same kind of thing in the gold mine or while walking on hills.

From an early age, my mum allowed me fairly free rein to walk where I wanted. On some occasions, I would find my way along a footpath to cross the railway lines.

There I would look, then touch or put my ear to the rail to see if I could detect the vibration from a possible arrival of an oncoming train.

When I was sure it was safe, I would go on to look along the banks of the river Beult.

Often I would see fish and the occasional otter. I just enjoyed investigating things without any thought of explaining where I planned to go or how long I could stay away from home.

A few years later, while still at Streete School that stood behind Hubble's grocery store in Headcorn, Dad often took me with him in his work van in the summer holidays when he could, where I experienced other enjoyable and certainly less frightening events, including riding in the cabs of steam and diesel rollers and having a go at steering them (with help but only for a short way that did not matter how well the road was rolled). Also of being on the back of a Barber Green machine as it laid fresh asphalt, as well as having a go with a pneumatic drill and a thumper—the latter taken quickly from my hands as it nearly stamped on my feet. I also had a few go at steering my dad's van in his work's yard. I felt I deserved some reward as I also helped him to measure recently asphalted roads to check the charges made by the company that did the work, Dad's job being that of a highways superintendent for Kent County Council.

If he could, he would stop at a café for a cup of tea and, for me, a bun as well—a treat that I always looked forward to.

Oh, those were happy and interesting days, as he was always at pains to explain exactly what was going on and why. I think I learnt a lot about management and organisation without really knowing it then. This experience was something that stood me in good stead when much older, partly because I never heard him shout at anyone, and only quietly give advice if he saw something that he thought was not up to standard.

This was how I was also treated when in primary school.

We also spent many Saturday afternoons in the front room of a house belonging to the village sub-postmistress, with its joint role as a sweet shop (and erstwhile illegal bookie) watching horse racing on TV in the semi-dark, while hearing the till ring from time to time through the adjoining door. I always won more money on the Grand National than Dad did, as he would put a couple of bob on my choices for me!

I sometimes wondered whether there was any other reason why my dad was always welcome, but I never thought to find out or asked him.

Other occasions that Dad took me to were Navy Days at Chatham, where he showed me the block he had stayed in while in the Navy, and to have a look inside destroyers and submarines as well as watch various displays on water. He also took me to a couple of Biggin Hill air shows and once to Farnborough where the Vulcan was by far the most impressive aircraft on show, with its steep, roaring climb up into the sky. (Many years later I returned there on business, as my company supplied graphics to one of the stands.)

About this time our dog, Wolfe, decided to worry sheep in a nearby farmer's field. My dad came home a little bit early to explain this and that he would have to be put down. Of course, I was unhappy at the news but also realised it was something we had to do. So Dad drove me, with the medium-sized dog on my lap to the vet.

I carried him into the room for the injection to be given and held him while it happened.

Of course, I was upset as he was very much my pet, but he took the injection quietly.

I don't think Dad could have done any more to show me something of the world around us.

Although Mum never forced me, she often asked me to help her with some aspects of cooking, so I gained a little useful knowledge for life later on.

Another kind of useful experience came from being in the school cadets where I managed to rise to the rank of lance corporal—just a tad higher than being an ordinary cadet.

This gave me a few odd experiences to look back on that I did not realise how much help they were for my later life, not that it was ever spectacular.

On the first summer camp, I tripped and cut my knee on an iron spike attached to a large tent. I went to the doctor for treatment and was surprised to find that the person treating me was someone I saw regularly on What's My Line on TV—Dr Reginald Webster.

Another couple were at Cultibraggan Camp near Comrie in Scotland. The first was when first using the latrines. The building had a central corridor with fabric sacks hanging down from wooden crossbars to hide anyone sitting on the walled toilets. These were most unusual as they consisted of quite high (for the youngest cadets) upright pipes with round wooden circles of wood to sit on, for excreta to drop into larger pipes running the length of the hut on both sides.

A friend, Colin Osborn was quite short and very thin so; when he tried to sit on the bowl, his bottom simply slipped in, legs waving in the air.

Unfortunately, for him, the toilets flushed once an hour, and on this occasion, someone had put some surgical spirit onto a crunched-up piece of paper at the starting end and set it alight. It came down with the tide just as Colin slipped in.

He came out faster than he went in, something like a champagne cork popping out of the bottle.

Another incident was when we were taken for training on the Perthshire hills and ordered to charge in a line. Colin was next to me as we ran forward, but when we were told to lie flat, we noticed that Colin was missing and went back to hunt for him. He had fallen down a small hole above an underground stream as he ran!

Not long afterwards we were taken higher and told to get into a trench. Below, we were told, was a howitzer.

Then we were told to keep down as shells screamed over our heads to thud into the ground further behind us.

Another camp was on a small island in the Menai Strait near the Menai Bridge. From there, one day, we were taken to RAF Valley, where we were given a ride in an Air Sea Rescue helicopter.

I was last to board the final flight of the Wessex and found myself sitting opposite the open door and the only one without a harness and nothing to hang on to!

The ride was quite exciting, particularly when we flew over Holyhead and the pilot tipped the craft so that I could see the tops of ships in the harbour through my feet, the only thing holding me in was centrifugal force!

Another incident was when we were in a camp near Chessil Beach. Apart from rowing craft across the inland water, on a day off a group of us went down to Weymouth beach, where one of our number, Bloomfield, put a white pillowcase on his head and a white sheet around him and started to call out some Gaelic sounding words in a nearly musical way, while the rest of us knelt and bowed up and down murmuring something like oooh-la, oooh-la and similar sounds.

We collected quite an audience who were told that this was an annual ceremony. Some visitors were invited and even joined in—and then were left there, as all but our 'priest' remained.

It gave us a bit of a chuckle to watch until the visitors realised that the ceremony was no such thing.

The last odd event was when a group of about twenty of us volunteered to be the enemy against the rest of our contingent the following morning.

We had to walk a few miles to the 'enemy camp' and spent the night camped in a disused farmyard on a slope. The tents we had were called tents the Arctic and had one open end, a floor and three sides and were built to accommodate two. We tied them down on a slope, with the closed end pointing downhill, facing the wind.

Unfortunately, rain began during the night, and despite having dug small trenches above the open ends, our tents proved to have porous rooves and watertight bases, soaking us and our belongings in the process. So we spent some of the night in a rickety barn.

It was sunny at dawn, so we put all our clothes on a fence running next to a small lane with a bridge over the stream next to the farm.

We were all completely naked and standing around while eating our breakfasts outside on a dry surface close to the road when, through the woods on the other side of the stream, came a minibus driven by a nun, with another one next to her on the front passenger seat. They were seemingly oblivious to our nakedness as they crossed the bridge and stooped by the open gate to the farm. The nun in the nearside seat opened her window to ask our nearest lucky one, Bloomfield again, for directions.

Before he could try to help them, the nuns suddenly became aware of their teenage schoolgirl passengers clambering over each other to have a look at us. So the driver shouted at her companion to say, "It's alright, I think I know the way," and started the bus moving again while shouting back at the girls to sit down and look the other way.

But, of course, they didn't but instead waved at us, while we waved back at them until they disappeared from view.

Coming back from my schoolboy memories, at least I thought, when he died, Dad had seen his eldest son married, my eighteenth birthday pass by, and he knew where I was going and what I was going to do when I left school and hopefully had pleasant memories from his past.

Shortly after he died, I received a letter from De Beers once more. It told me that visits to two coal mines had been arranged for me: one at the Victoria Colliery near Stoke during the spring holidays and the other in July at the Betteshanger Colliery in Kent, all travel and accommodation paid for. Not bad, just to see if I could cope with being in confined spaces.

During the Easter holidays, I travelled to Stoke and stayed at a hotel for one night.

The morning after my arrival I was collected at a reasonable time to go to the pit. There are few memories of the mine, other than I was given an overall to wear before going down two thousand or so feet in the main shaft.

The only actual event I recall from my underground adventure was of going down a vertical travelling way styled on a spiral staircase. There was a central column made from the natural rock and, right next to it, a rail track and beside that stairs carved out on the outer edge of the spiral shaft.

Why that remains a memory was from halfway down the travelling way. There was a sudden very loud rattle and banging from above and then, rushing and bouncing noisily past us around the bend, a couple of small metal tubs, seemingly out of control and full of coal, heading towards the lower shaft entrance where they would be pushed into cages to take them up to the surface to be unloaded.

I found it hard to believe that they did not fall off the track and injure us as their inside wheels seemed to lift off the rails a little as they passed.

Anyone going to the Beamish Museum would have seen what a working face might look like although, in the Victoria Mine, the seam we went to see was fairly level, and quite dusty although not being worked at the time.

During the summer, I was able to enjoy a couple of games of cricket for my house team at school, and a number for my village seconds, if not scoring.

One Whit weekend, when I was still thirteen, there was a friendly with a nearby village team as our opponents. In this match, I achieved the best bowling figures I ever got—six wickets for eighteen runs using my donkey drop style of off-break bowling. (For at least half of the wickets the batsman simply did not bother to play at the ball, as I bowled it to pitch about three feet outside the off stump, only to turn at about ninety degrees and hit the off stump, much to the batsmen's annoyance—particularly as it was a young boy bowling.)

In my last two years at school, I also did a bit of navigating rallies for a colleague of my dad's.

These Maidstone and Mid Kent car rallies were not that frequent but exciting nevertheless: strapped in as though in a fighter plane, in a full harness around my waist and over my shoulders, helmeted and sometimes bumping along narrow, twisting, tiny country lanes at seventy or more, in a souped-up mini complete with internal roll-bar.

Once, in darkness and fog on Romney Marsh, only seeing a T-junction sign moments before we had to turn left, I called my driver, "Turn left—NOW!" Handbrake on and steering wheel spun in opposite lock, we skidded to turn left at right angles, so that the underside of our mini was seen from a similar car that was just behind us but, instead of turning, it found itself going straight into the ditch opposite.

We also went on an economy run for Fiat and were based for the twenty-four hours at a Rolls Royce body building garage in Bromley, supposedly trying to achieve the best mile-per-gallon measurements we could.

Apart from a friend of my regular driver nearly turning over a Fiat 500 on a corner in Sevenoaks, when we were supposed to be going at less than thirty, I spent a night sleeping in the back of what was going to be the Maharajah of Jaipur's Rolls Royce when the bodywork was finished. It was surprisingly comfortable.

My exams were taken; there was a visit to the coastal Kent pit. Apart from it being under the Channel, leaking a bit and very dirty, particularly when one of the faces was blasted near us, my main memory was of three French girls who were somehow included on this visit, as well as a few other boys of my age.

Before going down, we were asked if we had old clothes to wear, all but the girls, who had arrived a bit late from Frances and wore light-coloured summer dresses, said yes. Unfortunately, for them, there was no alternative clothing available.

They were certainly pit black when we emerged from the mine, but I didn't see them after we boys had showered and left for home.

Having informed De Beers that everything had gone well, I received an order for my trunk that I still had to buy, which needed to be sent during September, and was told that tickets for a flight to South Africa in early December would arrive soon. They also arranged a visa for me to work in South Africa.

I just managed to pass my A Levels and spent the remaining time working as an estimator for a company in Paddock Wood, making pre-fabricated buildings, like offices or small homes.

As the time to leave began to approach, I started to realise that South Africa might be a strange place to live. Apart from anything else, it was extremely unusual to see anyone black in Kent. Even when I occasionally stayed with my brother, who lived next to Earls Court, London to go to see the Radio Show at Olympia or just look around a bit of the city on my own, or once being taken by my sister to see 'Stop the World I Want to Get Off', with Antony Newly and Anna Quale at a London Theatre. Even when Mum and I visited my dad most weekends when he was in St Bart's for a major operation, a black person was hardly ever encountered.

So what would they be like in a country with Apartheid? I didn't even know what Apartheid really meant then.

However, I had learnt how to be a member of a team, look after or encourage people, organise things, identify and solve problems, and I had a sense of direction. These were small ideas necessary for my and anyone's future life.

The end of October arrived, and I had to almost empty the house of all my possessions to cram them into the brand-new trunk that had to be sent in advance of my journey. My remaining clothes, such as there were, were everything I would have to wear for my journey, and to put anything else I might need to wear before the trunk arrived, in the one, quite small, suitcase that was all that was allowed to be taken in those days. Thirty-two pounds was roughly the weight of my baggage allowance. What it contained and what I wore on my journey had to be enough to last me for the next three months before my trunk would arrive in Welkom.

Before all that, there was a problem getting my passport as my mum had signed the application, but the Passport Office wouldn't accept it as it was not by my dad. He had died shortly after I had my job offer, so was not on hand to provide the correct signature. Then only a father could sign for a passport application, so later my mum had to send a copy of the death certificate to enable her to be the signatory.

When the passport eventually was approved and arrived, I put it away in a safe place. So safe that after three days of hunting through almost empty drawers neither I nor my mum had discovered its whereabouts. Even by the morning of my travel, when after another hasty but thorough search of all the likely places, we still couldn't find it.

To get to Heathrow in time, I had to catch the 9:30 train, so I set off down the slope to the station with my suitcase with hope but no passport. However, about two hundred yards from home, I suddenly realised that I had put it under paper lining in one of the drawers in my bedroom, and ran back for it.

How I hoped to get to South Africa without it, I don't know. Perhaps it's my eternal, though often misplaced, optimism.

As I travelled on the train up to London I wondered what it would be like; both the travel and the country. My mum's memories were from back in the 1920s so did not give me a very clear view of what to expect.

I had only been abroad once, and that was to France on a school trip. That memory flashed through my mind, and I was reminded of our arrival in Ostend when we boarded the coach and were informed by our teacher that this was the first time that this company had taken a school party from Britain, so we had to be on our best behaviour as the company's owner was driving. He was also a former Grand Prix driver.

That was noticeable when we careered through Clermont Ferrand, the wheels of the coach seemingly over the edge of the twisty mountain roads of the once range of volcanoes, with sheer drops of hundreds of feet visible as we could look straight down from the coach windows. The speed seemed unnecessarily high too, particularly given the narrowness of the road.

It also reminded me of our campsite in the Dordogne valley near Souillac that was overgrown with long, unkempt grass. One of our teachers went back into the village to get the mayor, who returned on a bicycle, with a scythe over his shoulder, to cut the grass before we could set up our tents.

However, while the teacher was away, one of our numbers needed the loo, so in he went to the small, rusty corrugated iron-roofed shed, with just enough room for one. Then from inside came cries of anguish, as he pulled the chain and got completely drenched from the deluge that cascaded down upon him, from the tank in the ceiling above.

I also remembered the night we went to see the son-et-lumiere at Rocamadour, the word being repeated and repeated over and over again, in a sing-song kind of way, throughout the light performance.

We were also taken to the Lascaux caves, to see the ancient wall paintings of animals being killed by brave warriors, and other red-brown images from that time.

By the time I reached Charing Cross station, my memories had disappeared to be replaced by being equally excited and scared. What would it be like? I'm flying from the same place the Beatles flew from, but there would be no farewell greeting from a rooftop crowd for me.

I quickly had to lose those thoughts as I needed to navigate my way to Victoria coach station to catch the service to Heathrow, and then to find out where to go once I got to the then small terminal.

Excitement and anxiety built as I waited to board our flight, but then there was an announcement that the flight would be delayed because of a fault in one of the engines.

Eventually, we were called to board the SAA 707, an hour late at around 4:30 pm. Then the engines were twice started and shut down for more repairs that were eventually fixed.

Apparently not, for an extra hour was spent on the apron of Zurich Airport sitting in the 707 waiting for further repairs.

When eventually our flight landed again, we were allowed to stretch our legs to visit a dilapidated wooden shed, in the middle of what otherwise appeared to be a deserted field that looked a bit like a bar seen in Westerns and served as a kind of transit lounge at Las Palmas airport.

Later, when it was already light, we landed again, this time at Luanda, but because, also being a military airfield, no one was allowed who was not leaving the plane—or to take photographs.

Then on to Salisbury and the excitement of being buffeted by lightning storms, wings waving hello to anyone watching and threatening to send a present to demonstrate the power of a jet engine to the inhabitants below, as we approached the airfield. This thought resulted from my having recalled the nasty habit of the 707 to throw off one or more of its engines in such conditions.

Finally, after 25 hours, we eventually touched down, three hours late, at Jan Smuts, Jo'burg.

A cousin of mine, Mary Strick, whom I had never met, was there to greet me. She was looking rather annoyed by the delay, and so she hurried me to her car and on to the railway station entrance in the city for my overnight journey to Welkom in the Free State. Fortunately, I had the ticket with me and was just in time to board the seven o'clock sleeper.

It was an odd experience organising sleeping arrangements and getting ready for bed with three complete strangers in the four-berth compartment—one of which was for the wife of one of my fellows.

I was awoken at about 5:00 am that Saturday morning, by the train slowing and stopping for no particular reason it seemed, before going on to the station serving the African township outside Welkom not long after dawn. I had already changed while the others were sleeping and was sitting on what was once my bed, looking out of the window.

As we drew in I was astonished by a sight that I had only seen on film or television; what seemed like hundreds of black Africans in tribal dress, stamping their feet and ululating as well as waving shields and banging spears on the ground or waving knob-kerries in the air. Yesterday, I had been in the twentieth century, but what year was it now? Are the native Africans always like this? Had I done the right thing? Like it or not I had to get on with it—there was no turning around and going back now.

We continued to Welkom proper, where I was collected from the whites-only station, and taken to Protea House by someone from personnel. It was like a large red, brick-built hotel and down a bit of an arcing drive.

Before he left, the person who had collected me, seemingly unaware of my journey of two days to get there, asked if I would like to go to the mine after I had found my room.

I was so tired, thanks to a baby crying most of the night, and a bit hungry that I thought breakfast and sleep would be best, so I declined. It was Saturday after all, and he had told me that it was just a half day at work, so it didn't seem worth the effort.

The staff at Protea House were lovely. The lady manager showed me my room and other facilities quickly and then took me to the dining room for something to eat.

The cost of staying here was something over thirty Rand a month—the equivalent of fifteen pounds back home then. For that, you had a centrally heated bedroom with washing facilities and a built-in wardrobe that was cleaned every day, a shower and toilet block for each floor, as well as a large dining room where you could eat as much food as you wanted.

For example, it was not uncommon for my evening meal to consist of fresh fruit juice, soup, fish, lamb cutlets and vegetables, a quarter chicken and more vegetables and a large steak with yet more veg, all washed down with orange squash. Then I might have sponge pudding, ice cream and fresh fruit, followed by cheese and biscuits and coffee.

After my breakfast, I had a quick look around the buildings, noticing a large sitting room to my right as I left the dining room, around the corner the entrance and waiting area, then through a door to the right I went out into a large quadrangle with three blocks of bedrooms around the sides opposite the dining room, each with gardens in front and, in front of them, a path roughly circling a grassed area, within which was a small swimming pool and a number of tall trees.

That was enough for me, so I went back to my room for a good rest.

Anyway, after a lovely sleep, I woke about lunchtime to find workers from the mine returning for their lunches.

After I left the dining room, I just sat in the reception area for a while, until a couple of people came in and sat down beside me. They were obviously cricketers judging by the bats and bags beside them, so I asked them who they played for. It was my future team!

After some chat, they asked if I would like to come and watch. How could I refuse?

The rest of the weekend was something of a blur, but I remember getting a lift to the mine on Monday morning.

That was after a normal sort of English breakfast and just before 8:00 when my contact from Saturday picked me up to take me to work on Monday morning.

The mine seemed a long way out of Welkom itself, but it wasn't that long before we turned right onto the private road to the mine itself. We passed a road to our right, and through the line of poplar trees, 1 Shaft was pointed out to me. "A bit further over there's 1A Shaft, too," my driver told me.

Eventually, we parked up just beyond the offices on 2 Shaft. "Here we are," my driver from personnel declared as he stopped the car, and we got out.

Nearby were the shaft top buildings, and beyond that, you could just see the top of a great grey mound of waste rock that had been brought up from underground and, in front of it, the black Africans' accommodation block.

The man from personnel took me in tow, through the main entrance and down a corridor to the surveyors' office. I felt a bit overdressed in a sports jacket, shirt and tie, and grey trousers, as most of the people I saw walking around were in shirt sleeves or safari suits.

Firstly, I was introduced to the chief surveyor, of whom I saw little and hardly spoke to him again in my three years or so working for him. Although I often saw him just sitting looking at maps in the glassed cubicle of his small office just by the entrance to the L-shaped main office, there was not even a raised hand given to any of his staff. He just seemed to like being on his own.

Only on very few occasions, he did speak to anyone and that was when he thought he had found a fault with their work—never with me, though—or if there was something important to do.

Then I was taken on a whistle-stop tour of the rest of the building by one of the senior surveyors, Lyle Estment, who was also captain of the mine's cricket team, before returning to my future lair to have a cup of tea.

Lyle was always cheerful and kind and loved his tea, I discovered, for not only did he have an extra-large mug of his own in the office, for when the tea trolley came around, but he also had a habit of following the trolley to another one or two offices to get even more to drink. This happened three times a day, and how he managed to sup it all and hardly go to the toilet, I never discovered.

Anyway, after being shown around a bit, he tried to describe what it looked like underground from the maps he showed me. However, without seeing the operations underground, it was not easy to follow exactly.

After a lunch of packed sandwiches from the kitchen at Protea House that I had been told by my breakfast companion that morning to take and the essential cuppa, I was introduced to some of my future colleagues as they returned from their work underground.

Then I was allowed to watch the process of them sitting down at their desks and, almost silently, calculating their results, before entering the locations of new pegs on the different maps of stopes or other developments. The only time they seemed to talk to someone else, was when something didn't work out. Then, usually, a number had been entered in his calculations incorrectly, or something quite simple like that.

It was a good job I had learnt and liked trigonometry, as this was something I would later use daily until a computer was bought for mine.

It wasn't like the ones today, as it occupied a large office to itself, with another office next door with about thirty people putting data onto punched cards, that were then run through the computer for it to make the calculations that us surveyors no longer needed to do. I'm sure they did other things as well but, as it was rare to go anywhere near the building again, I don't know what else they could have been up to.

Gradually, I gained an impression of the work I was to undertake, but the reality of the task turned out not to be that simple or safe!

At the end of the day, I was advised to get some appropriate clothes to wear, as I was to be taken on a familiarising visit underground the next day.

So when I got back to my new home, I managed to cadge a lift into town to buy some, as well as a safari suit as this was near the peak of the summer season, not that it got very cold in winter.

During my time living in Welkom, I only saw snow once, but then it was brief and didn't manage to lie.

I also found out where my assigned doctor was based, and how to get back to my base on Shanks's pony. It was nearly half a mile, and I passed the mineworker's club that was quite close to home and would later become an important part of my leisure activities.

The next morning, as I was having breakfast, I saw one of the group who had taken me to watch the cricket on Saturday. He came over and asked how I was getting into work, then offered me a welcome lift.

I don't remember his name, but he told me it would be easy to get a lift to work as half the people living at Protea House worked at President Steyn, the rest at President Brand, the neighbouring mine.

It was strange that, before I learnt to drive and had a car of my own, only one of the close friends I developed at Protea early on worked at my mine, and he was a shift boss, normally going underground on three shafts, half an hour after those on the other three shafts but well before the offices, so he was normally of little use. He was also a bit of a Romeo, so didn't always have time for one of our often lavish breakfasts.

Anyway, he was kind enough to drop me at the offices, before going on to his destination that morning.

However, I was soon offered lifts by some of my surveyor colleagues or found that I could easily get a lift from somebody, even if I had to hitch a ride from someone going past Protea's entrance.

Almost as soon as I got into the surveyor's room, Lyle approached me.

"Have you got the things you need?"

I nodded.

"Then get your cuppa."

The trolley had just arrived, and he wanted his drink of tea before leaving for the shaft. "We'll need to go fairly sharpish because I have arranged for us to get a cage in about twenty minutes."

I hardly had a chance to finish my drink before being whisked off to the changing rooms. Fortunately, it was only a few minutes' walk away.

The place smelt a little of garlic and a light body odour aroma but not too bad. It was also very tidy and clean despite the number of people who had been there earlier, judging by the fact that nearly all of the meshed wire cages, that passed as lockers, were full of everyday clothing basking in the sunlight coming through windows almost all around the room and above the yellow painted walls.

Most of them had padlocks holding the belongings of the regulars, while the others were not guarded in this way. They were for those who, like us surveyors, were itinerant workers.

Despite this, I never lost anything, even money, from them during my years in the mine.

Anyway, we were quick en route to the shaft, me with a borrowed red hard hat, normally the sign of being a shift boss, and Lyle in grey.

On the way, we stopped at the lamp room to collect hat lamps with attached black rectangular batteries that could be clipped onto our trouser belts.

Arriving at the shaft I noticed what looked like a very large, round, red brick chimney nearby.

"That's the ventilation shaft," Lyle told me, "There is a cable down it, but it is only used for inspections, or available in a dire emergency, but then it is next to useless for that purpose as there's just a big bucket that travels very slowly."

"Ah! Here we are." The three grey metal decks of the cage emerged from underground, "We go in the bottom deck. The upper two decks are for the black miners and for carrying materials, such as new trucks, cables, and dynamite. This deck is also used for the same things when miners are not coming on or ending their shifts—it's also important to remember when the cage will be coming for your return to the surface or you might be waiting a long time," he chuckled.

In this case, we shared the steel shell with two small red-painted wooden trucks full of explosives. At least they weren't sharing the space with detonators, we were assured by the cage's conductor, or more correctly the bellman.

Slowly, the light of the sun disappeared, but quite quickly we accelerated to a speed of around thirty miles an hour vertically.

It was surprisingly smooth, and after about two minutes we were slowing. The lights of the first station passed us by, soon followed by a second, then a gradual brake until we stopped precisely at level 42 (4,200 feet below the surface).

The bellman pulled up the steel roller shutter and ushered two people out, before himself leaving the cage and then, after removing the trucks of explosives, ringing the station's bell to signal to the winding engine driver that the cage could move on to its next destination. That was after a short delay for the bellman to get back in after first locking the gate to the shaft.

Then we went on down to level 45 where our destination lay.

When I stepped out, I was surprised by the cavernous size of the station compared with those in the coal mines I had been down. The entrance to the travelling way must have been around thirty feet square and sloping from around forty feet high down to ten where the haulage proper started.

The shaft itself was so large that it allowed the two adjacent 'lift' shafts for men and machinery, two more for the express rectangular 'buckets' carrying rock to the surface, and one for the Mary Anne (a slow-moving small cage for people, powered separately from the others, so that it could be used in an emergency, or when the main man cages are being checked or serviced).

The shafts, then, are enormous compared with those in British coal mines.

We walked towards the well-lit haulage carrying a single-track railway, with a small ditch on one side by a walkway, although when there was no moving traffic, men also walked along the track itself.

My first impression was of a uniform grey granite rock around me but, gradually, I was able to see how beautiful the rock actually is. It can sparkle with fool's gold and tiny red, blue, green and dull yellow crystalline dots. Occasionally, we passed nearly vertical faults that had a kind of black or, more usually, white quartz, cracked like crazy paving by the violent force of explosions when the travelling way was being excavated.

I discovered during my time underground that fault lines could be anything from a couple of inches to one or two feet wide, but rarely were there different strata on a show that would allow you to see what the slip might be. (The slip being the difference in height between identical strata of rock that may have been moved up or down maybe millions of years ago.)

Remarkably, the rock seemed to give off its own vague smell, sometimes augmented by the smell of warm dampness and rotting wood from old wooden props in worked-out stopes. It really fascinated me in a way that almost every time I went underground was somehow mostly an enjoyable experience. Only when ventilation was poor and the air almost still, with tiny grey particles of dust just floating there and only moving as it swirled around me, did I not enjoy the journey.

I looked down into the drain beside us, "Why is there almost no water and why is it what there is travelling towards us?"

"There's only one stope still working on this level and only a very small fault draining into it. And you might notice that the haulage is going very slightly uphill—intentionally of course because we need to drain water out of the workings, and the slope also helps trains pulling trucks full of rock to travel more easily back to an orepass or boxhole next to the shaft, where its load is dropped down to the bottom level—from where it's then taken up to the surface."

"That seems a bit odd. It's not like the coal mines I've been in where the trucks themselves go into the cages to be taken to the surface."

"Well, although it may seem a bit of a cost to drill mini shafts from the different levels down through the next, it's much easier to manage the waste and ore-bearing rock, and it means that the big buckets can travel up and down very quickly, perhaps fifty to sixty miles an hour, and almost continuously, from just one level. So while there's an initial cost, doing anything else would be very inefficient."

"I hadn't thought of that."

"Right, we're here," Lyle gestured left into what he called a crosscut.

The rails branched into it as it curved left under the reef.

Again Lyle pointed to a concrete structure on our right, a now unused rusty metal chute protruding from it, its mouth blocked by an iron door. "That's where the rock is dropped into waiting trucks," he explained. "The tunnel above is called an orepass or boxhole—either will do. It's a bit like a well when you look down it from the stope and usually has a criss-cross of rail lines across the top to stop very large rocks or people falling down it."

In front, we encountered a large black and yellow striped door, surrounded by light grey breeze blocks that completely sealed the tunnel.

"Push it open," Lyle commanded, almost laughing as he said so.

I pushed, thinking it should be easy, but it would hardly budge. Lyle just chuckled at my discomfiture.

"These doors are as airtight as they can be. Blocking them allows air to be circulated around the mine more efficiently. It's just the force of the air pushing from the other side that can make it hard to push open sometimes."

Lyle lent his weight to mine, and we managed to move it and get through, only to be confronted by a second such door with the same purpose and problem.

Now, apart from the lights on our helmets, we were in complete darkness.

As we turned right, the roof got lower, so we had to stoop to go further. After about another twenty feet, the footwall suddenly dropped, and we found ourselves in what is known as a raise.

Lyle explained that this was how a stope started: all raises followed the reef from one level to the level above and would be connected to a crosscut at each level, then the reef would be gradually mined outwards from this central corridor.

"How does the rock get removed?" I asked.

"Well, if you look a little below us, you will see the top of a boxhole, linking to a concreted exit structure at the bottom like the one we saw in the crosscut just now," he said as we went about eighty feet down the raise to see it. Just before reaching it, he pointed out a winch, "That's what brings the rock to the boxhole. There's normally another one put in much closer to the face when a stope is approaching its furthest development, or about to go into its neighbour. That is smaller and used for bringing down rock from the face after firing. Of course, the slope takes quite a lot of effort to remove the rock."

On either side, as we descended were what looked like boxes of wood, not like the single upright round props I had seen in the coal mines back home. These were about three feet square; having two about six-inch diameter logs in one direction with two on top near the ends of the first ones with alternate gaps between them until they reached the hangwall (the rock ceiling). To stop them rolling, they have groves cut out near the ends to slot into the log below. If necessary, smaller, flatter pieces of wood would be forced into any gap between the round logs and the hangwall to help stop the roof from collapsing.

When I pointed this difference out, Lyle explained that there was sometimes only a few inches of granite above the hangwall until a layer of shale. "Shale is very slippery and can easily break through and cause a complete collapse with the single props used in coal mines. Being a deep mine, there's a lot more pressure, and whereas coal is the nearest thing to shale in being slippery, the roof above it is normally very stable, so there is usually very little risk of a rock fall in coal mines. Whereas, here it's a different matter. In some parts of the mine, the shale is so thick, and the distance between the reef and shale so small that the shale gets mined out first to avoid such tragedies."

"In that case, the granite-like rock, containing the reef, can be as little as eighteen inches high, whereas mining here the distance between footwall and hangwall is normally thirty-four to thirty-eight inches."

"You'll get a chance to see both types of stope in the next couple of days."

I thanked him for the explanation then realised we were almost at the boxhole's edge.

It wasn't that easy to see the hole itself as it was criss-crossed by pieces of used railway line that stopped very large blocks of rock falling down and blocking the exit at the bottom, Lyle reminded me. Then of course it was dark black, even with my lamp looking down at it.

"Not that large rocks end up here very often. Usually, if rock of that size is seen near the rock face, it gets drilled into smaller pieces before it is pulled out," Lyle concluded.

"Now I'll show you our part in the proceedings," Lyle shone his torch onto the hangwall. "There's what we call a peg. (It was a small, round metal plate, with a U-shaped piece of metal that had a hole in it for a bob to be attached when surveying.) Each one is numbered and follows on from another peg behind us, at the end of the crosscut. This way we know how deep it is and where it is, so it can be plotted on a map. As you've been shown, each stope has its own map or plan."

"I won't complicate things for you now but up to that point," Lyle said, pointing back to where we had entered from the crosscut. "Everything is horizontal, but when we enter the positions on a stope's plan, like the peg here, the distances are calculated as they are on the slope."

"I'm sure I'll understand it properly when I do it for real," I replied.

"Good! The only other things we do are put pegs into the tunnel that the miners make slightly in advance of the faces they are mining. These tunnels are called ATCs or Advanced Track Cuttings. These are put in every eighty to a hundred feet or so, depending on the slope and other geology affecting the reef. You can see the two ATCs here." Lyle pointed each side of the top of the ore pass to the passages going slightly diagonally up the slope into the gloom.

"It doesn't look as if they've been working here recently as they are clear of rock and there is no winch cable either."

We entered one of the ATCs, and as we walked, Lyle pointed out more pegs still secured to the hangwall.

"The pegs are then used to measure, as closely as possible, how much rock the miner has mined out each month when we measure up then draw the picture of the new face on the stope's plan—and that determines how much he gets paid. It also ensures that one stope doesn't accidentally get mined into its neighbour. So it's quite a responsible job."

"I see."

"From that, the mine management can calculate roughly how much gold we should produce every month—but you'll find out all about that when you do a short stint in sampling."

I nodded.

"Right—we'll go down into the working part of the stope now."

We turned and went back into the raise.

"By the way, we also put the pegs into haulages and crosscuts as they are cut. Again this is to make sure that such developments go in the right direction," Lyle mentioned as we made our way back.

We turned and started to descend the raise, stepping cautiously past a completely open boxhole, then turned right along another ATC and walked along to its end, then entered the top of the lower east face. Here it was a question of a crawl or spider walk as the roof was no more than three feet high.

When we got a few feet in and close to the face itself, Lyle pointed out another peg.

"If you look down the face you might be able to see another peg in the ATC, or perhaps you won't," he chuckled when it couldn't be seen. "But you'll find it when we're down there."

"Anyway, to measure the new location of the face each month, we just put a tape measure down from the peg at the top to one in the ATC, then measure the distance to the face every ten feet and write it into our notebooks—simple really."

"This enables us to draw the new position of the face on our maps up top, and clearly see how the faces in every working stope have advanced."

"Copies are sent to the Mine Captains on the different shafts, so that they can understand both the effectiveness of the different miners and look out for any potential problems, like accidentally drilling into a neighbouring stope."

"If faces do get too close to one another, one side is shut down so that the other can be safely mined until all the reef is mined out."

"Now I understand the maps of the stopes and their purpose better, and just how important our work is," I told him.

That was basically the end of my lesson.

Next, we sort of slid down the face to the bottom and then back along this last ATC in this stope and into the raise to walk a little further down and leave the stope in a similar way to the way we had entered the level above. Then we went out through a doorless crosscut that allowed fresh air in, and on to the station to await our cage.

"You may have noticed that the raises between levels are not necessarily at the same angle as the reef varies as it gets deeper, so the stations are sometimes three hundred feet apart to take account of this. Usually, though it is a fairly constant two hundred."

Looking back on it, this was just about the longest conversation I ever had with any surveyor about work or life underground.

Most of the time, of course, I would be working on my own with my little gang of black workers, but even in the office, no one ever seemed to speak about anything that they had seen or experienced underground. Any trauma anyone experienced was suppressed or got rid of later with a strong or prolonged drink.

This was an unwritten rule that I only became aware of as time went by.

Back in the office, we went over the plans for both 42/46 and 45/46 to see where we had been.

After lunch, Lyle took me outside to practice reading angles and measuring distances.

I was eighteen and had only been in South Africa for a couple of weeks and was standing in a grassy piece of sandy scrub behind the offices, learning how to use a theodolite in the still, warm afternoon sunshine when, suddenly, I was aware of something on my left wrist, and absent-mindedly flicked at whatever it was. The presence seemed to have been dislodged successfully when I took my flicking hand away.

But no! There it was again. I looked at the creature more carefully; it was a very tiny black spider on the underside of the wrist. There was nothing to feel but, taking no chances, I took careful aim and this time my flick disposed of it.

I had only ever heard of this sort of thing but never expected to experience the results for myself, particularly from one so small.

I returned to what I was doing and thought no more about it, just taking sightings to where Lyle pointed, then reading off the angles, both horizontal and vertical, while recording them in Lyle's notebook. It was quite easy, and I soon had the gist of it.

It was only when we got back to the office that I took a casual glance at my arm and was surprised to see red marks creeping slowly up my arm from where I had flicked the spider off.

Remembering images of poisonous spiders from television that always seemed to be fairly large with long legs, I thought nothing more of it and got on with my mid-afternoon round of tea.

I was very busy during the rest of the afternoon plotting angles on a blank sheet of paper. There was no itching or anything to make me look at my arm again. It was only when I got back to my room at the mine hostel and took a shower that I saw that the red streaks now extended up my arm and across my chest. This was a bit alarming, so I sought advice from a new-found friend, who immediately offered to drive me to my doctor's.

I was surprised how quickly the doctor recognised what was wrong—even before I told him anything except my name. His only question was whether I had been outside in the veldt.

Within minutes he had gone to his medicine chest and brought over a glass of water for me to take the two little white tablets he gave me.

"Come back at the same time tomorrow," he instructed. "It should be better by then."

There was no discernible change when I left for work in the morning—my arm was a little swollen perhaps but nothing more. However, by the time I got home again, my arm was a grey-white flabby thing.

Someone else offered me a lift into town to see the doctor again, where I presented my appendage to him as soon as I could.

"Ah, good! Take your top off and just put your arm out, wrist up."

I did as instructed while Dr Bolell went to a cupboard and took out a white porcelain pudding basin, along with a scalpel.

The bowl was placed on a wooden chair in front of me. He took my arm and told me to keep it still, my wrist facing upward above the bowl, then a quick swish with the scalpel across the sagging skin on my wrist.

No pain as, when he slit my wrist, I could see that there was quite a gap between the outer expanded skin and underlying tissue. Then he quickly turned my arm over, and with both hands circling around the top of my arm, he pulled down towards my wrist.

It was just like watching someone squeeze a gigantic toothpaste tube, as the white puss, streaked with red, erupted from the slit he had made, half-filling the basin.

He repeated this once more to make sure most, if not all, of the blood-spattered gunge was out of my arm.

"There we are," he exclaimed as he did a second pass. "Let's just clean it up and put a plaster on, then you can go."

That was easy, I thought, *but how did all that come from one little spider?*

Then he bandaged my wrist and sent me on my way with an instruction to come back if I noticed anything strange happening, otherwise to keep my bandage on for five days. "Then everything should be okay."

Sure enough, my arm had healed up by then and there was no sign of any flab, so I was fit enough to start a short period working in the sampling office, almost next to ours, down the corridor.

I had a few days alongside a regular sampler watching and practising taking samples of the reef.

This was quite interesting at first because the thickness of the black reef could vary so much: from a thin black line, hardly distinguishable against the surrounding rock, and perhaps less than a millimetre thick but at least more or less straight, to something over a metre thick, with pebbles of a mixture of dark grey, black and white with black streaks. This, I noticed, depended on which shaft we went to, the thickest being at the lowest levels on Three shaft which, at that time, could be about eight feet thick or even more in the stopes on this shaft.

However, fortunately, I was kept away from this shaft as it was only the very experienced samplers who were given the jobs with the thick seams to sample.

The stopes could vary in height too. Some could be quite low: between thirty-six to around forty-two inches high when the roof could tolerate it, but when there was a small distance between the reef and a wide thickness of soapy black shale above, it was necessary to take this out first before removing the rock containing gold—in this case, the stope could be ten or eleven feet high.

I was given a chance to try out my skills of chiselling out a handful of rock, including the important piece of reef of course, at various points down a face. Then putting each sample into a small bag to be taken to the sampling office where it was labelled, then sent on for analysis.

What was surprising to me was that the value of gold might be as little as five or seven pennyweights: around a quarter of an ounce or about seven grams of gold for each ton of rock removed. (Its value in 2020 would be roughly £250 to £350 per ton of rock of about 12 cubic feet in size or about a third of a cubic metre.)

My experience the first time I sampled on my own was quite unexpected.

I had only been at the mine for two weeks and just had one stope to do.

As I entered the crosscut, I saw a strange sight. On the back wall was a large picture of Jesus carefully lit by a lamp above it and in front was a lectern, with the top of a Bible just jutting out above the rim. But more astonishing, for this naive eighteen-year-old, was a white miner hitting one of his black workers about the head until his circular metal hard hat, shaped a bit like an upturned jelly with a rim, fell off.

The hitting stopped as I got closer, and both looked at me strangely, mouths slightly open, as I approached. What was also a bit odd to me was seeing the black worker calmly bending over to pick up his hard hat, and walking away as if nothing had happened.

When I got close to him, quite innocently I asked the miner, "You've got a picture of Jesus," gesturing to the lit picture and turning to the lectern with a black Bible on top, "…and it says in the Bible, 'Do unto others as you would have others do unto you', and here you are hitting him," or something to that effect while pointing at the back of the departing worker.

"Ah! Sautie" (a crude, slightly rude, word for an Englishman), he spoke almost defiantly in a rough Boer way. "He's a kaffir, not even a human being, he's less than an animal," as his way of justifying his actions.

47

I now had my own grey plastic hard hat, so he understood when I told him that I had come to do some sampling. There was nothing else I could or would dare to say to this large and intimidating creature in front of me, so I just got on with the subject of my visit.

"The faces you want to sample are all clean." (Not being drilled or cleaned of loose rocks.) He turned dismissively and opened his red box where, I later learnt, he would keep his food and whatever he might need during the day—plus explosives when they were delivered later in the day if he was blasting.

I certainly didn't want a confrontation or some kind of difficulty on my first solo effort, as I guessed that there could easily be some kind of accident if I wanted to argue with him. However, I was pleased that my unexpected appearance had stopped the possibility of serious injury to one of his workers.

So I just got on with my work, with that racist memory that will stick in my head until I die.

Fortunately, his was a normal kind of stope of about 30 degrees to the horizontal although it is none too easy to break out a small section of reef with a hammer and chisel, when you're on your side and on a slope, and the ceiling or footwall could be only a few inches above or below your swinging hand. The only good thing is that because of the force of explosions to break up the rock that had been in front of where I was sampling, the rock on the face was slightly cracked and reasonably easy to chisel out.

This contrasted with the situation in a stope when the fairly soft and slick shale is removed first, then later the greater part of the force from firing the gelignite within the gold-bearing rock goes up instead of forward because there is nothing above it. Then the gold-bearing rock that then comprises the face is almost unaffected by the gelignite exploding, so the low face is left remarkably smooth.

Trying to dislodge the millimetre-high reef that I needed, then required a significantly greater effort than in a normal stope, whose face often has minor cracks nearby as a point where you could aim your chisel.

The fact that the reef is well below you, also means that you have to be a bit of a contortionist to get in a position to use the chisel, particularly as the rock face is slippery and very hard so much more difficult to break out.

The only saving grace was at least you can stand upright afterwards. I didn't really like the work, but my sampling days were soon over, thank goodness.

Then I just needed a couple of days accompanying a fellow surveyor to know exactly what to do.

After Christmas was over, I was let out to go on my own, with my own gang of, fortunately, well-trained workers to help me: a boss-boy, a general assistant who carried my theodolite in its wooden box but who had charge of two others; one older man who carried the tripod for the theodolite to stand on, plus a piccaneen (as his position sounded when spoken about although the Oxford English Dictionary has it as piccaninny). His job was to carry everything else, including spare clothing sometimes and my lunch and a bottle of ice cold—until it got warmed—sugared black tea, all supplied daily by the canteen at Protea House. I can't remember when or how my Christmas at my mum's sister's home in Johannesburg was arranged, nor how I got there, but it must have been by train and taxi. Anyway, I arrived on Christmas Eve, just a few weeks after arriving in South Africa, and was introduced to some of my relatives on this side of the family for the first time although I had met my aunt and uncle when they visited us the year before. The others were descendants of theirs, including my cousin, who was Anglo-American's company secretary. Fortunately, they only stayed for an hour or so as they had their own family Christmas preparations to complete.

On Christmas Day itself, I had Christmas dinner with just my aunt and uncle. I didn't see it being arranged and was surprised to find I was being ushered outside to have the meal.

Again memories are vague, but I do recall it feeling very strange eating a Christmas dinner, just like at home but sitting at a table in the shade of a peach tree, in just a white safari suit that I had recently purchased. A tweed jacket and long trousers are not that desirable in the middle of summer.

The meal itself was just like what my mum always prepared. The only odd thing was being invited to put my hand up to pick a peach to eat after finishing a normal Christmas pudding and white sauce.

All too soon I was back in Welkom and the routine in the mine.

Taking charge of three other people I did not know, and only had Fanakalo: a mixture of English, Afrikaans and black African tribal words, with which to talk to them.

Nevertheless, I did have some understanding of management and teamwork from cricket, being a member of the school cadets, though never having a rank above lance corporal, and particularly from my observations of how my dad managed the people who worked for him.

Looking back on it, it was something of a surprise how well I did manage, and it is only now when writing this that I really understand the value of the experiences above to me later on in my life.

This was something that also helped me when I was teaching management at college, as I was aware that, like me, many who I taught did not realise what skills and understanding they had learnt from life, rather than the subjects they had taken, or not, at school.

What being an underground surveyor was actually like:

Apart from the last one, the following events did not happen in any order that I can remember, except the last few, but all of them are still clearly etched into my mind.

Mining gold in South Africa, compared with the coal mines in England, is very dangerous. Safety rules were never explained to me if they ever existed. The only one I did know was that smoking was not permitted but try saying that to most white miners who largely ignored it. You also had to be prepared to expect almost anything to happen when trying to get the job done.

What was very surprising to me, looking back on life at President Steyn, is that nobody ever talked of the kinds of experience that I had although, in retrospect, I find it hard to believe that I was the only person to have experienced the type of incident that seemed to follow me over the forty odd months I worked there.

One example was one day when I needed to travel past and above a fairly recently developed orepass in order to get to the part of a new stope where I needed to put in some pegs.

This particular boxhole was unusual because, a it only had one side to get past it, as a significant fa to the hole on the other and was almost glassy sheer and had no solid hand or footholds that were usable.

Probably, at least in part, that was the reason that a quite large piece of the roof had collapsed above the boxhole; the weakness at one side possibly being enough to bring down a substantial amount of rock above the orepass when blasting it. Anyway, the space was not unlike that of a shaft at a normal station, other than there was a roof above it, and it wasn't quite so big.

What it meant now was that I would have to traverse an almost sheer wall of rock, with only a narrow ridge above me to cling to, and a slightly narrower one for my feet to use. So, as far as one could, pressed against the face, and without looking down at the twenty-foot drop, possibly followed by another of over a hundred feet down the boxhole, me and my boys had to negotiate this obstacle for about twenty-five feet—not very far if you say it quickly.

At least I didn't have to worry about carrying anything, unlike my team who followed behind me, my boss-boy with the theodolite, Madulla, the oldest with the tripod, and particularly my small piccaneen carrying everything else. I even remember crossing my fingers as I looked back and watched them.

When at last I could look back at the empty scene, it seemed to remind me of a great grey funnel, offering little hope of survival if any of us slipped and fell, because not all of the criss-cross girders, to stop large boulders going down, were yet in place.

At another time, I needed to put in a directional peg in a small raise. It was only there to mine out a small block of reef that had been created between two nearby faults that had somehow shifted this block upwards.

To get to the bottom of this short raise, I and my gang had to go along a disused ATC in an old stope and follow a horizontal tunnel of similar size, from where one of the faults had forced the small bit of seam upwards.

This passage ended where a boxhole emerged from the haulage below. Its top was simply an unguarded black hole going down a hundred feet or so and about seven feet square that must have been used to eject waste rock from further tunnelling, one part of which we needed to get into.

To get from the passage, we were into the new, short raise, we needed to use another horizontal tunnel, about four or five feet wide, turning at right angles to the one we were on.

Because our passage was also four to five feet wide, there was a corner jutting out between the two tunnels, leaving us with no direct path to use. So getting from one tunnel to the next, which had a slight upward slope at its entrance and was set back about six inches, required a short leap of faith to jump and grab the rope, that was hanging down from an iron hook, fixed roughly in the centre of the top of the boxhole, and swing round, holding on with both hands, rather like being on a funfair roundabout without the horse to sit on, and to hopefully land at the bottom of the next tunnel 'and' stay there.

I can still remember my leap of faith and a slightly sickening uncertainty in my stomach as I wobbled on the receiving edge. Fortunately, I just managed to grab something solid with my right hand while still holding on to the rope with just my left. That then allowed me to stay on the ledge instead of going back; probably into the gaping hole that was now waiting behind me.

I was first, both up and down, and had to catch hold of my boss-boy's shirt to stop him from falling back when he was next to follow me. He then followed my example by catching the rest of my gang, after taking the various objects they were carrying and which they passed to him around the corner.

After that, putting in a new peg and a direction marker cross on the face of the then short new raise, which started about fifteen feet from the boxhole we had traversed was a doddle but also had its problems. The only thing different from usual was having to have my theodolite fairly close to the footwall in order to focus on the peg in the roof at the top of the boxhole that we had just managed to get over. There was no way that I would ask one of my crew to try to hang a bob from it, nor was I inclined to try and measure its distance from the peg I was under, and of course, there was the rope hanging down just by it that was likely to have got in the way anyway. At least the distance and difference in height between the peg at the top of the boxhole and the one I was under was unnecessary as it was already known. I just needed to record the horizontal angle to it, though it was a very unusual practice not to take the other measurements to be sure there had been no movement in the rock since the one I was under had been put in.

The only way to do this was by splaying the tripod's legs like a spider's, with the top of my theodolite just below my knees.

Then, to observe both the boxhole, peg and mark the location of the new peg for my boss-boy to put in and then take measurements of the bob hanging from the peg that he had put in, I had to contort my body on the ground, while avoiding the tripod's legs and also knocking or moving the theodolite from its position directly below the peg I was measuring from as I moved round it on my bottom.

Because of the age of the theodolite I was using, I also needed to look down from above to read the horizontal angles and from the side of it to read the vertical angles for each peg, which made the task even more hazardous as there were small pieces of broken rock on the footwall that might make me slip on and make me accidentally move the platform for the theodolite. Even if only slightly, it would still mean setting up the equipment again and taking the measurements once more.

Then I had to move to be under the new peg to use the theodolite again in order to put in another peg further up the raise and also mark a cross on the face for the miner to use as a guide to blasting, but this time, I could use the theodolite at its normal height which made this part of the exercise seem very simple.

Having the two pegs in place and the face marked allowed the miner to use bobs of his own from each peg to align the angle of incline of the raise himself so that he could further develop it but, as ever, adjusting it if the angle of the reef changed. (It would then require another peg, put in at a later time if there was a change of vertical angle in the reef.)

This was all good fun, and nowhere near as easy as my practice sessions with Lyle, my colleague and cricket captain, and a couple of others led me to believe.

Anyway, the measurements I took allowed me later to calculate both the horizontal distance and the change in vertical elevations on a plan back in the office.

Remarkably, me and my three crew members successfully managed both the entry and exit over the unguarded boxhole, in the same swinging way.

It was not that unusual to have to go past an unguarded boxhole when going down a stope but at least then there were usually wooden props near or beside such an obstacle to holding on to, and a bit of rock in between to stand on too, as you went past, not like the one we had just had to cross.

A couple of months after Christmas I heard that the then Prime Minister, Hendrik Verwoerd, was going to speak at a rally at the town's football field. Having never seen a live rally by any politician, let alone a Prime Minister, I thought I would go along to see what it was like.

I hadn't expected the size of the expectant crowd when I got there and had to be content with just seeing his head and shoulders, with the occasional hand gesture above their heads, when he got going.

Unfortunately, he spoke only Afrikaans for the most part, but I could feel and hear the eager response of virtually everyone but me, as he continued with his oratory.

I left early but was impressed by the way he spoke that had his audience listening avidly, his voice was almost like a rousing piece of music to my ears. It was just like going to the theatre but this time having real meaning rather than some imaginary historic event.

Later that year, he died at the age of sixty-four, two days before his sixty-fifth birthday.

Going back to a kind of funnel top to a boxhole, there was another one in my story, a bit like the one mentioned before but this time in a stope and just below an ATC. Going back to the kind of funnel-topped boxhole, here it was more like the end of a trumpet with one of those round caps on top that trumpeters use to make a wah-wahing sound on the instrument. This image was created by the three tall, wide towers of pit props, about eleven feet high and positioned on the three sides other than that of the ATC where I was standing.

The edge of boxhole's top was about four feet to my left and a couple of feet down. About two feet below that, there was a criss-cross of rails made from shortened, used railway lines in order to stop any large rocks going down that might block the chute going down to the crosscut around eighty feet below us.

Where I was standing was a lot of loose, quite small rock. That made it quite tricky to stabilise the tripod under an existing peg and get its top level ready for me to use. Eventually, I managed it, then put my old-fashioned theodolite on top and centred it directly beneath the bob. I signalled to my boss-boy that I was ready and bent over to try to sight the bob hanging down from the new peg that he had already put in, close to the ATC's face in front of me.

Because of the loose, broken rock underneath me, I was gripping on hard to the tripod to stop it from moving, as I lined up the small telescope on the bob in front. Then I heard a winch start-up, seemingly somewhere not very far away. Unusually, I hadn't noticed one near the beginning of the ATC, as normally is the case, so that its operator can see down most of the tunnel's length to be sure there are no people or obstructions that might cause its scoop to snag.

Because the winch had a muffled kind of sound I guessed that this one was a bit closer to me than my boss-boy but probably being used for another ATC, or the raise itself.

There was no warning shout or anything, so I assumed that there was nothing to worry about when it started up. I soon found out that my assumption was not to be relied upon.

Suddenly, I felt the stones beneath me move slightly, and with no further warning, the hawser, attached to the scoop that I could see just my side of my boss-boy, sprang up out of the small rocks below me with some force—right between mine and the tripod's legs—throwing both of us unceremoniously arcing left into the air. An amusing sight, no doubt, to anyone watching, but certainly not for me as I became aware of being horizontal for a short time, but long enough for me to notice and take a snapshot in my mind, of the wooden stack of pit props bizarrely, apparently vertical rather than horizontal, as it would be normal to see them, before I started to plunge head first down towards the latticed top of the boxhole, my hands gripping the top of the tripod as hard as I could as if my life depended on it.

My nearly eight-foot aerial drop finished in such a way that my head disappeared under the criss-crossed used rails, only stopping because the parallel rails were close enough to catch my shoulders. Had I landed ninety degrees the other way, I could have missed the rails completely, as they were further apart than those that stopped me.

However, that did not stop my hard hat, which somehow managed to detach itself from its lamp and my head, as well as the tripod, with its theodolite still attached, disappearing down the boxhole, as they were loosened from my grasp when my wrists hit a rail and jerked them out of my hands. Then, as I lay in a crumpled kind of position, I heard the pieces clatter and bounce down the sixty or seventy feet or so to the bottom of the boxhole.

I don't remember my legs landing on the rails, but I do remember that there was a short pause while I assessed my predicament and found a rail with my feet that I used to somehow right myself in an uncomfortable kneeling position, then get my bearings, before getting up and gingerly traversing the potentially slippery grid to safety.

It took a short while to realise exactly what had just happened, as I just stood there for a moment, before cautiously climbing the short step up from the lattice of rails to the ATC, there to be greeted by my worried team looking at me and asking if I was okay.

Still shaking a little, I sat down opposite my erstwhile sudden grave to have a swig of ice cold tea from my flask that my piccaneen had thoughtfully handed to me and tried my best to gather myself together.

It was only after the drink that I became aware of my shoulders hurting a bit and exactly what had happened to me. Then beginning to shake some more as the realisation of the close shave came into my mind: imagining what falling down a dark, rocky tunnel, angled at sixty degrees to the horizontal, head first might have been like, if I survived the bouncing and bumping that long.

Only then did I begin to really appreciate the concern that my little team had for me. It felt somehow different to the way many black Africans might think of their boss, perhaps because I was generally very appreciative of their endeavours, treating them more as equals than black servants. The only exceptions were when one of them did something thoughtless, or potentially dangerous, when I would get annoyed (as I almost certainly would with anyone else).

Anyway, the loss of my theodolite put an end to my surveying that day.

All I and my boys could do was go down to the crosscut at the bottom of the stope, a hundred or so feet down the raise, and look to see what we could collect.

When we emerged into the crosscut, I took the opportunity for another sit down while my piccaneen, the smallest of my little party, with the help of my boss-boy, managed to climb up onto the metal chute at the bottom of the boxhole, open its hatch, clamber in over some loose rock, and recover the bits that were left: the top of the theodolite with its little telescope that had been separated in the fall, the tripod, a little battered but with the theodolite's base still secured to it and my hard hat that had somehow been dislodged from my black, plastic covered lamp that now hung limply beside me on its cable.

Breaking the theodolite was great because the broken one was ancient and very fiddly, but the new ones had a small, lit-up eyepiece that clearly gave all the information needed, instead of being like my broken one, where I had to read the angles of two silvery arcs of metal with pointers against them, one round the base for the horizontal and the other alongside the telescope for the vertical angle.

When I returned to the office and presented the pieces to my immediate boss, all he did was complain that he would now have to find a new theodolite for me. He didn't bother to ask me how I was.

No one else asked me what happened, just giving a little chuckle as they saw the debris. I may as well have thrown the theodolite down the boxhole instead. Just why I didn't think of doing that before, I don't know.

It is only when writing this that I have asked myself an obvious question: why on earth did they drill a boxhole halfway along and next to an ATC? I never saw such a location anywhere else in the mine. It would be hard to suggest that anyone would have done it just for my benefit!

Not only was almost nothing about accidents and incidents usually talked about in the office or with colleagues, but I never heard any conversations of the sort from other people who lived at Protea House. It was so strange. I was sure that others must have had the odd close shave because, on average, one person a week died and there were a number of non-fatal accidents.

Most of the time my life was not endangered, and I spent most weekends playing either cricket or hockey, with a couple of evenings practising and trying to keep fit.

Cricket matches were played over two Saturdays with Sunday usually being a lazy day but sometimes swimming in the pool at Protea House. It was shaped a bit like a kidney and not that large and only existed after someone, a few years before, had blown a hole in the grounds for fun.

As far as cricket was concerned, I began by playing for the Mine's second eleven, attempting to bowl medium fast and do a little batting as well as I could. This was until I was asked by my colleague, Lyle, to join the first team because of my catching and fielding that were my strong points. Strangely, after trying to bowl off breaks in the nets, as I did when playing for Staplehurst, I was occasionally asked to bowl them for the Firsts.

The bonus for playing cricket was the free afternoon drinks, cricket tea and sometimes a game of darts at an away ground, or a party or dance in the evening after a shower and change back home.

This was because the younger members used mostly to hang out with each other.

To my surprise one day a colleague, who I didn't know that well, asked me if I would meet him for a drink in the evening. It was odd, not only because we had rarely spoken before, and I didn't think we had much in common; nevertheless, I agreed.

I had no idea what he wanted, but he seemed anxious to talk to somebody. Perhaps he would have a tale to tell and might listen to some of my near misses as well.

He was already in the bar when I got there, and seemed to have something troubling on his mind but just asked if I would like a drink, which I agreed to. But, when he asked me and I told him what I wanted, he replied that I should try a cocktail instead of the lager that I asked for.

Anyway, when he came back with my cocktail, which to me seemed rather too potent, I just accepted it. Then I asked if everything was all right. I remember him rambling on about something meaningless to me, and when he suddenly stopped he downed the remainder of his drink, got up and without asking, told me to drink up and went for another different, lethal mixture.

This went on for an hour or two, he neither spoke about work nor his family, but I suspected that one or both were troubling him. Certainly, the drink was troubling me, so I excused myself and left before I fell over. Still unaware of why he had sought my company.

The trip home, had many trips as I was very unsteady on my feet but somehow I managed to wobble and crawl myself to get back to my base and, with difficulty, unlocked my door, when I almost fell in.

Never again, I promised myself. Not that I was asked again, nor do I remember him speaking to me unless it was directly connected with a job I had to do.

Back at work, even if I glanced towards him sitting at his desk, he appeared to avoid me, so I still don't know what that night was all about, but later, I heard that he had had a problem at home.

To some extent, I was grateful not to have to undergo his generosity again.

The only time any conversation about feelings relating to home or work occurred was when someone had measured up a fatality one day, and then only once and very briefly. Coincidentally, I had witnessed an intermediate part of the incident that led to his gruesome job.

Now the surveyor was busy chatting to a small group of us about what he had seen when he went down the shaft.

This brought back the memory of that day of going down the same shaft and walking along haulage with my crew, and shortly after turning a corner about a quarter of a mile from the shaft, we had just descended, then heading towards a stope that needed some new pegs. As we rounded the corner of the crosscut's entrance to the stope, there came a black African running as hard as he could towards us, his eyes seemingly popping out of his head as he charged headlong towards the station. He ran past us apparently completely oblivious to our presence and then, as I turned to watch him behind us, he ran out of sight.

"What was that all about?" I asked my boss-boy whose English was pretty good.

"He is probably being chased by Tokaloshi. He must have done something that caused him to see the spirit in the rock—perhaps when he was drilling—and it's chasing him for whatever he has done."

It seemed as reasonable an explanation as any, so we just continued our journey and finished our work as if nothing had happened.

Back on the surface in the office, I was just finishing my calculations prior to plotting the pegs' locations on the stope's plan, when the colleague had come in. As the crowd started to gather to listen to him, I naturally joined them.

It turned out that he had been sent down to measure up and record the location of any signs of the fatality—the death of the man that my team and I had seen running, who had subsequently run full tilt to the station and jumped into the shaft to escape the spirit.

The only unusual thing my colleague had to impart from his report was that he had found the man's penis, on its own, lying `on a girder near the bottom of the shaft. Anything else about the man's demise was left to our imaginations.

Recalling this incident reminded me of the advice I got about most of the black workers in the mine. I was told that they were still very tribal, as witnessed that first morning looking out of the train window. Killing a member of a rival tribe was not even frowned upon, let alone would the South African police do anything about it, particularly as they were almost all Afrikaaners and didn't much like white Brits let alone blacks.

I understood from my well-educated boss-boy that, in their villages, the local tribal chief was responsible for any punishment. The worst crime that a tribal member could commit was to steal from another, when there was a possibility of losing a hand at least.

Talking to black workers was also frowned upon, whether in Protea House or underground. I was often shouted at for chatting to my boss-boy, but as a fluent English speaker, I liked to hear as much as I could about the black Africans' way of life: what they believed in and where they lived.

As these conversations were almost always interrupted, and my boss-boy feared the consequences for himself, I only found out a little of his life; his family, the fact that there was a different kind of Apartheid in other countries, like Malawi, where he was in the wrong tribe to take on responsible or professional jobs, he told me, when I suggested that I could teach him how to do my job if he wanted.

Most of the black mining gangs working on the face were led by members of the Zulu tribe, being the best educated, upper-class black citizens, whose word among the other tribes was law, or certainly appeared to be.

The workers below them were almost as afraid of them as they were of the white miners in overall charge.

The longer I stayed working in the mine, every day I seemed to wonder if I was going to be killed or injured—it could be anywhere at any time, even when you were still on the surface.

These thoughts brought back my memory of the motorcycle deaths when I was young. Who, in those days, would have expected anything like that?

Anyway, getting back to the theme of this part of my story, even in Protea House some strange and remarkable events could happen that hardly merited a mention either, if at all.

The first event that I can recall was one sunny public holiday when I was looking out of my window across the quad, and I saw a strange-looking group of people with a suited male leader and about eight grey-haired women in summer dresses, emerging from a door on my right.

At this very same moment, I heard a gunshot, then another and another as a couple of inmates started to fire blanks at each other across the quad. (This was not uncommon and must have happened five or six times while I lived there.)

However, it certainly took our visitors by surprise.

There were a couple more shots and then silence, apart from a man who suddenly yanked open the glass entrance doors to the block opposite me, and ran as fast as he could across the quad, shouting and waving his arms about him, with a green and yellow towel wrapped around his waist which was flapping as he ran.

The small entourage continued to move sedately across the quad as if nothing unusual was happening although, judging by their faces, they were somewhat bewildered by the events around them.

But, when the towel inevitably fell from its place of covering, the ladies appeared even more unsure where to look, as he ran right past them, seemingly not aware of their presence.

Shortly after this, I heard wet sounds of running feet and shouting from somewhere down my corridor, then a door being flung open with more shouting following it.

Unfortunately, I couldn't hear what followed, and all noise gradually dissipated.

Later on, I discovered that this mini battle had been pre-arranged after an alcoholic agreement the night before, but the man in the towel, who I had never seen before, was not part of it. Neither was I for that matter.

The fact that the group of Anglo-American shareholders were going to be visiting at the same time was also unknown to them.

The reason for the man in the towel rushing across the quad was also revealed to me a bit later: he had just entered his room after taking a shower when a live bullet had come through the window of his room and ricocheted around him. Consequently, he was somewhat livid at the unexpected encroachment by the ballistic intruder. The end result was there for all to see.

There was also an event that occurred in Protea House roughly every six months, on the night after those learning to be miners heard that they had passed their 'use of explosives' tests.

This always occurred in the early hours of the morning, usually about three o'clock, when some person or persons, who had purloined some articles from the subject of their training, stuck detonators in all the door locks down the corridor, linked them together with a fuse, and simply let them off bang, bang, bang getting louder and louder as they approached my room, when the locked door would be unceremoniously blown open. Then the now louder bangs continued to the last room.

I was always surprised to find mine, and all the other doors down the corridor, still in one piece, with the lock in the locked position but still working as if nothing had happened. Even the door jamb was seemingly unaffected.

I still marvel at the explosions' lack of damage.

One of the small groups in Protea House that I was part of had a three-monthly ritual that I was asked to join.

This was to give blood—something very necessary in Welkom because of the number of accidents that occurred.

However, I'm not sure that what we provided was really what was wanted, as we always had at least a couple of lagers before making the donations.

Another of my close escapes happened when I was putting in a peg at the top of a face, itself being at the top of a stope.

The trouble in this situation was that not only was the ventilation poor, but the face itself was developing almost diagonally upwards as well, meaning that there was almost no fresh air where I wanted the new peg to be, as its location needed to be within this unventilated triangle.

In any event, it is already quite hot when you get a mile below the surface, and often my clothes would be sopping wet with sweat within a couple of hundred yards of leaving the station.

This situation was even worse than being in haulage because at least there was always some movement of air that you could feel, but in this corner, there was not a breath. I remember counting my heartbeat at over 150 beats a minute because of both the fact that the rock itself was warm, and because of the lack of ventilation, there followed a lack of oxygen, and I was beginning to feel a bit dizzy.

Of course, I didn't put the peg in myself, but my boss-boy was calling for help, so I had climbed up the face from the ATC below and was close to and just a bit below him. It turned out that he had called for my advice because he had found that the ideal location was in a weak area of hangwall and was seeking guidance about where he should put the peg because I would need to sight it from below and yet it needed to be fairly near the face where the weakness was.

We agreed on what we thought would be the best place, and I was beginning my descent to the ATC, where I had left my theodolite when, as he was attempting to hammer his auger into the roof, to later insert some rounded wood for the peg to be hammered into, the hangwall started to give way.

Immediately, I heard cracking. I shouted for him to get out.

For me, the only way to escape was to continue to go downhill to the ATC below as fast as I could, as the roof was beginning to split above the only route downward I could take. So I shuffled and slid as fast as I could downhill, on my bottom, using my hands as kind of paddles because there was a wall of wood pit-props between me and safety away from the face. Fortunately, I had already strapped on a kind of rubber sheet that saved my bottom from being hurt, as I tobogganed as fast as I could over the loose rock from the previous night's explosive excavation.

The explosion of the sticks of dynamite had probably been the cause of the weakness as, unbeknown to the miner, the hard rock above the reef had probably thinned, as it did sometimes, making it thin enough for the weight of slippery shale above to break through and, once started, to continue its way down behind me.

Occasionally I took a fleeting look back only to see an upside-down shower of black and grey rock and an accompanying cloud of grey dust, like an upside-down smoking tsunami of rock, chasing me and seemingly getting ever closer down the hundred-foot face, as I paddled even faster.

In the end, I almost fell over the lip of the quite deep ATC. My feet slipped and my knees almost gave way, but somehow I managed to grab my theodolite, which took just a fleeting moment, before I could run the five yards or so to safety below a square of slightly squashed wooden logs, valiantly holding up the hangwall there securely.

Behind me, the loosened rock almost filled the space I had left behind, the sight of it gradually dimming as rock dust began to fill the space between me and the site of my possible demise—another unremarkable, except for the time, event in my life.

There was no more to do here. My boss-boy had put everything he needed together and brought his gang down to see if I was okay. That being so, and there being no chance of completing the work here, we went off to complete putting in another couple of pegs in a different stope, as if nothing had really happened.

Once more, this escape failed to merit any conversation among my colleagues, or even my friends back at my lodgings.

After all, there were any number of occasions underground when one or two large, or a number of smaller rocks, might have fallen down just where I, or anybody else, may have been standing just moments before. Any one of these events would have ended in death or serious injury, but these were always dismissed as a hazard of the job.

I can't remember the number of times such events happened to me, but it was certainly many more than just a few.

Sometimes the rock produced some very, to me a mere novice underground, odd results from movement.

Quite often in the oldest parts of the mine, instead of movement from above, when walking along haulage, one might see the wall showing signs of being broken by pressure from the side; and rock jutting out with cracks almost from top to bottom as though a book had been partially opened. Another surprise to me was that occasionally the footwall would be forced up by the pressure at these depths, twisting and bending the railway tracks up by six inches or so.

One particular oddity was in an old, worked out, and now unused stope that I and others used as a travelling way from one level to another.

I don't remember exactly when or why I used this particular stope to go down a couple of times in the same week.

The stope in question was one on One Shaft where the shale had had to be removed, giving it a height of eight to ten feet. This meant a nice, easy way through as there was no need to bend or duck under any rock overhead.

The first day down I was able to stand up with the hangwall well above me. But a couple of days later, I was astonished to see the smooth grey granite roof had bent without any signs of breaking.

I remember stopping a couple of times as I went down simply to check if what I was seeing was right, and asking myself how such a solid stretch of stone could suddenly act as if it were plastic.

At its entrance at the top, its height was much the same as earlier in the week but, as I descended, the roof got lower and lower. So much so, that I had to bend, having an almost horizontal back to get through a short stretch of the raise, even though the part of the raise I was going down now had a kind of gully about eighteen inches deep.

More remarkable was the sight of a nearby, once very strong-looking winch, that originally had a drum nearly four feet high and was now about half that height. The seemingly sturdy packs of pit-props at this point were also splayed out almost making a continuous wall of sticky-out wood.

However, by the time I reached the bottom, the ceiling was back to the same height as back at the top. I recall shaking my head and looking back up the raise, just to be sure that what I had encountered was really true. How on earth can a seemingly solid granite-like rock bend as though it was plastic? I wondered, and still do—it still seems impossible.

There were a few times when I and my team had to use an unexpected route to leave the place where we had been working. On one such occasion, to leave the stope, whose lowest part had been pushed up by an ancient fault, exiting entailed going down a boxhole that was being transformed into a travelling way.

Firstly, there was a short downward incline to a corner, where the tunnel turned at right angles and carried on down the now disused boxhole at an angle of about sixty degrees to the horizontal. It was not very high, perhaps four or five feet, and very roughly mined with a rock sticking out a little from its roof and walls. Only the footwall was fairly smooth, meaning that a metal equivalent of a rope ladder was necessary for anyone to get a footing as they climbed or descended.

When I got to the corner, I could see a small group of black workers, right at the bottom, digging away at what remained of the broken rock from the stope above, to clean out the section just above another turning leading to the crosscut below. I suppose that the total descent would have been about ninety or a hundred feet.

I went first, as usual, and soon found out just how necessary the chain ladder was because sometimes when I put my boot down to find a rung, it would slip before being caught by the next metal rung below.

Anyway, when I was just above the black workers, some sixty or seventy feet from the turning above, I looked back to see if my gang were following.

At the turning, I could see my boss-boy. I don't know whether something made it give way or he knocked a very loose rock that I had not noticed, but he yelled at me, "Watch out baas," as a boulder about two feet wide and four feet or so high, began tumbling end over end banging, towards me.

I turned to look down at my potential escape route. Most of the digging gang had heard the shout too and were scrabbling about, trying to leave the scene at the warning.

Unfortunately, the boy immediately below me had got his foot somehow caught up in the ladder and was making futile attempts to release himself. On either side of him, there was still some loose rock that blocked any potential escape route for me.

So I just turned to watch the oncoming grey acrobat tumbling towards me.

The travelling way was about five feet or so wide, and the rock moved from side to side as it tumbled, each time following my attempts to jump out of the way of its new route. How it knew that I had changed position and when to follow me, I just don't know, but this three-quarters-of-a-ton solid grey coffin shape seemed intent on my destruction.

When it was about ten feet away, I stopped my little dance and just watched; thoughts of escape gone as I prepared for the end.

I don't recall hearing its thuds or seeing any more after that despite still looking up at its approach, except for what seemed a very long and slow series of images of my past short life, particularly pictures of my mum, or having a bun in a tearoom with my dad when I was out working with him, opening Christmas presents, and many other events being screened in front of me. Everything felt so calm, so peaceful and serene: it was actually a strangely pleasant and relaxing experience. One that seemed to take a long time but, in reality, was little more than a few seconds. This series of images still come back to haunt me at times.

However, this kind of reverie was suddenly and rudely interrupted as I became conscious of the rock hitting the ground just above me, then rearing up towards the roof, its ominous, all-embracing grey wall quickly filling the whole of my vision. Then I suddenly felt something pushing against the brim of my hard hat. I remember shutting my eyes for no practical reason. Then my head went suddenly very calm, dark and wonderfully peaceful again. But then I was abruptly taken away from my passage to oblivion as I became aware of the rock now resting itself quite gently against my nose.

It was only as the reality of the sudden stillness passed through my mind that I became aware that perhaps my life had been saved by an unseen hand.

For a moment, I stayed still; then, as my mind became more focussed, I leant back and glanced up to see if the grey menace was going to topple further forwards on top of me. I may have managed a small smile as, reassuringly, it had come up against one of the pieces of rock jutting from the roof.

My mind went completely blank as I began to shake uncontrollably until I finally managed to think of getting out of my erstwhile tomb. How lucky, I thought again that I had been fortunate enough to have stopped just below my saviour rock, and not a bit above it.

All I remember of my exit after that was looking down to see if my route was now cleared, and briefly up beyond the rock for my boys to look down to see if I was okay.

I know I managed to scramble shakily out by myself, and into the crosscut to sit down against the rock wall, still shaking, because I was in that position when I saw my boys come smiling towards me, asking if I was all right, and then my shaking stopped as everything seemed suddenly normal again.

Any more of that day is missing. I assume that I went on as if nothing had happened, and then I just went back in the office and concentrated on completing entering the data I had collected onto sheets to be passed on to the recently completed computer block because then everything was put onto punched cards for the computer to read, calculate and print out for us so that we could plot all the data onto maps the next day.

However, the late evening when I had put out the light to go to sleep, I remembered just how calm and peaceful my escape from death was. It must have been a reaction to the thought that I was about to die.

Perhaps it was the same kind of thought my dad had when watching TV with me when he decided to go to bed.

Hopefully, he too had pleasant recollections of good times in his life before he died peacefully, I thought to myself.

The afternoons in the office were now quite relaxed, and we had time to chat—but not about anything much and certainly not my lucky escape because anything like that was taboo in this strange world, as I see it now.

The only real conversation was about where I, or others, might be going the next day—or night.

One of those days could be to do with measuring how far the working faces had moved forward during the month.

Those days were both good and bad.

The bad thing was having to go down with the miners at anything between four-thirty and six o'clock in the morning, depending on the shaft.

I hated going down among the (white) miners. Most of them were drawn from Greece, Turkey, and Germany as well as the Boer South Africans, and nearly all of them were overweight, were sweaty, ate garlic and drank lots of lager, judging by the low noises and various smells pervading the confined space in the cage, which held thirty to thirty-five of us.

This was made worse if I had also been to a party or just a night of drinking the day before. Apart from anything else, it could mean mistakes being made and having to re-do all the work again the next day, as well as that which had already been planned. Somehow, despite the effect of alcohol, I only had to repeat my work once, and that was after one very merry New Year's Day party which ended at the time I had to leave to go to the mine. Some others were not so lucky, and fairly regularly had to do the double dose.

However, the bonus of a measuring day was that, if the stope or stopes, were easy to get to and reasonably clean to get into and down the face, you could be on the surface again by ten and home as soon as the work was finished, as long as there weren't any complications when plotting the new faces on the plans.

The early finishes allowed more time to either practice cricket or hockey, which I had taken up after the cricket season had finished, or to have a drink in Jan Prak's room on the top floor of the two-storey block opposite the dining room at Protea House.

Jan's room was popular for two reasons: one that he had a wonderful hi-fi system and an interesting library of music to play but, most importantly, he always had a fridge full of cold lager. Of course, the small fraternity always contributed to his hoard.

There was another reason in the summer months as we played a little game of shooting the empty can, as it dropped to the garden below, having been thrown from his window.

This all went well for me until one day when a different revolver was being used.

The usual pistol had a two-movement action for the trigger. The first easy movement got the gun ready to fire and, reaching the small resistance, squeezing harder which let the thing go off at the appropriate time while following the can's flight to quite near the ground. I was well used to this, having been in my school cadets and fired a variety of different guns, gaining a marksman's badge in the process.

Unfortunately, the way this new pistol worked hadn't been explained to me when I was handed the replacement, so it fired straight away. So, instead of the bullet leaving the gun later when it would have gone into the garden below, it flew at a shallow angle hitting the surface of the water in our small swimming pool and ricocheting on to hit the brick wall opposite.

Unluckily, there were two people swimming in the pool at the time, who were very displeased, shocked and vehemently angry by this incident but fortunately unhurt.

I never took part in this little ceremony again.

Protea House was a strange place in some ways, as illustrated by the incidents above, but had to be praised for the food and service we were given.

For example, my usual breakfast was fruit juice, followed by a bowl of cereal, then eggs, bacon, tomatoes and fried bread or, sometimes steak and egg, followed by toast and marmalade and as much tea and/or coffee as you wanted. In addition, a packed lunch was available if needed, and you weren't going to be in the hostel during the day.

Our centrally heated rooms were cleaned every day and nothing was ever stolen, even if money was left lying around. The showers and toilets, though communal and at the end of the block, were immaculate.

Every evening meal began with soup, then fish, followed by three main courses that you could repeat or partake of all three if you wanted to (I sometimes ate all three if I was very hungry!) followed by a pudding, cheese and biscuits and coffee. There was always a proper Christmas dinner and lobster was the speciality on New Year's Day when wine was also on the menu. These special meals were always served in the lounge, which was bedecked with the usual kinds of Christmas decorations.

Not bad really for the equivalent of fifteen pounds a month.

Having an adequate supply of good food as well as plenty of exercise underground meant that it was easy to enjoy playing sports.

Although hockey was new to me, it was good to be with people with the same aim and language out in the open. What we had in particular was a desire to be the best. Though mostly a young inexperienced team, we decided that we would do better if we played hard, particularly as our team only had three or four older, skilled players. This included our goalie, who also played for the Free State team—he was certainly vital.

Most of our competition had skilled and experienced players. So we developed the tactic of always trying to have at least two of our sides opposing one of the other.

This could only be achieved by being very fit so that we could help each other out. So much of our twice-weekly practice sessions involved a walk, trot, and race programme, covering half to three-quarters of a mile before any practice of attacking moves. Our defence relied on speed alone from most of the team.

This tactic brought us more success than the preceding season although not top place.

In the 1967/1968 season, a new player joined the team. He was a recently qualified Spanish geologist who liked to be absolutely perfect in all he did. Unfortunately, his skills with regard to hockey were not that good.

If any of the opposition stole the ball as he was about to hit it, he would stop, stand straight up, raise his stick above his head and slam it into the ground, so that it bounced, and mutter some probably Spanish swear words to himself, before he could regain his composure and join in the game again as though nothing had happened.

On the other hand, he demonstrated that he was a good geologist, and set himself the task of measuring the thickness and composition of the reef, from South to North and West to East through a sample range of stopes from three to six thousand feet.

Why nobody had done this before was that the geology department had relied on results from boreholes that had been drilled before the mine became established.

However, simply looking at the reef in stopes and samples that were brought to the surface every day could have told anyone what the width and composition of the reef were like, but no one had pieced together this evidence for some reason.

It seemed that the geology department's main task was to know the location and movement of rock caused by faults so that mining operations could be better planned.

The result of the Spaniards' efforts was to show that the gold deposits had been laid down millions of years before when there must have been a very large river delta.

As with anything heavy, like a rock being pushed downstream, the largest and heaviest pieces of rock would drop to the bottom first, while tiny particles would go further out into the sea, even if, as in this case, it included gold, which is quite heavy.

As a result of his work, he predicted that there was more gold to be mined further north and east of where originally it was thought there was little gold to mine.

Consequently, three new boreholes were drilled that confirmed his predictions and led to a fourth shaft being sunk to a depth of seven thousand feet.

I never found out how the gold deposits had been found in the first place, but they extended for about twelve miles across and four or so from the nearest to the surface to the lowest.

Getting back to my sporting activities, cricket was a bit different to hockey as President Steyn's first team contained a large proportion of skilled and experienced players. The only benefit of having a few youngsters was their ability to field.

My particular skill was catching, so I was normally positioned somewhere close to the bat.

One day Lyle, our daemon leg spinner and captain, put me at forward short leg, almost within touching distance of the batsman, with the hope of getting a dolly off bat and pad.

However, Lyle dropped one ball unusually short and the batsman swung his bat and middled it, hitting me full in the middle of my forehead, knocking me to the ground, and looping into the air behind me and towards the edge of the field, where the batsman was caught by a colleague just in from the square leg boundary.

Still a bit dizzy, I reluctantly agreed when Lyle asked me to bowl the next over from his end. I thought he would be sending me to the outfield for a bit of rest instead.

I was never the best bowler or batsman but somehow managed to contain the batsmen at least, so I felt I did all right.

As a batsman, I was not aggressive or skilful enough.

I just enjoyed the game.

These reminiscences reminded me of one regular event while travelling to Kroonstadt to play either cricket or hockey.

En route, there was a T-junction where one had to turn right.

The road I turned onto was clear to see in either direction for about a quarter of a mile, when still a hundred or more metres away from the junction. Nevertheless, there was a stop sign with a wide white line to tell you to stop before turning.

Perched below some trees, on the hill to my right, there was always a police patrol car with an officer inside, who watched every driver through binoculars, to see if any driver could be stopped for crossing the white line without himself stopping, as that would produce a fine and, I guessed, some remuneration for the officer.

It seemed that this must have been a lucrative occupation judging by the regularity of my journeys although nothing was earned from me.

Mentioning Kroonstad reminded me of my mum telling me that her dad had been imprisoned there by British soldiers when he was the stationmaster. Presumably, they suspected him of being a Boer, judging by the name of the town, not of Scottish stock. However, when they realised that he was on their side, they released him.

Getting back to my life, I later trained and passed the cricket umpires' exam with certificate number ninety-seven, if I remember correctly.

With some experience in the local league behind me, I was selected to umpire a match between Orange Free State Country Districts and Witwatersrand University that contained three players close to selection for the national side due to tour England.

Unfortunately, their left-arm spin bowler, included in the later cancelled tour, dislocated a finger of his bowling hand when taking a return catch at my end.

Unfortunately, the tour was later stopped because of Apartheid.

Going back to life within Protea House, one of my neighbours and I were going out one evening, so went to the showers together. We completely forgot that there was a national school's netball competition going on in Welkom, and one team had been given various empty rooms to use around the hostel.

Anyway, as we were leaving the shower room, with only towels over our shoulders, we heard some girls chattering and obviously heading towards us. So, quick as a flash, we wrapped our towels around our heads, so we wouldn't be recognised, and walked past the obviously slightly embarrassed teenagers giggling as we passed, and got into our rooms.

There was one other incident there that I will never forget.

Jan was on holiday at the start of November, so two friends and I decided to have a lager or two on a first-floor balcony overlooking the street opposite Protea's main entrance.

While we were idly chatting about nothing in particular, someone none of us knew, burst onto the balcony and asked if he could have a lager.

A bit confused by his sudden arrival and the strange kind of curiosity he was showing for the road, one of my friends handed him a can.

Almost immediately, as we followed his gaze, there was a 'berdumph' sort of sound, and a small section of the road lifted up, followed closely by a spout of water and a delighted expression on the stranger's face.

Almost dancing in delight, he immediately turned and left the balcony, never to be seen again.

Apparently, he had just finished the use of explosives course and had managed to purloin a stick of dynamite and a length of under-water fuse that he must have lit to set the explosive off, after flushing them down one of the toilets, thus giving him time to reach our vantage point.

It was very odd, but strangely like many other events, the incident was never reported to the police and no investigation of any kind was carried out. It was just another day in this mining town.

It was yet another occurrence that no one talked about afterwards. We didn't talk about love or women, even if we knew anyone had any romantic liaisons. It was both a waste of time if we were loveless, and nobody wanted to share their secret if they had.

In this town, single women were outnumbered by single men by what seemed like a ratio of around one hundred to one.

As far as I knew, there were only a handful of the hundred or so men in Protea House that had any kind of liaisons with the opposite sex, and of this handful, only two of them—both of whom owned sports cars—had any regular success but whose partners were rarely seen.

Almost the only single women I saw, let alone met, played hockey. These young women may have been single but were rarely available.

I only managed one short partnership from this source and that was with one of a pair of identical twins. It seemed that they liked to play a game with anyone who they deemed to be possibly suitable, as they took turns to go out with whoever it might be, but I was not to know that and only found out after the following event.

It was during an evening at a dance that I had invited someone to come with me and I had a very odd experience. We were in the middle of the dance floor, trying to dance to a traditional tune. It may have been a waltz, but whatever it was, I felt a kind of rushing in my head, and then I suddenly found myself being transported up to the high ceiling and looking down at myself and my partner. I began to laugh at the awkward way, particularly I was trying to follow the steps, when I equally suddenly rushed back to my normal self, still laughing, although at first not realise it. It was a few moments before I saw a very bemused look on my partner's face and came back to reality.

I remember trying to explain what had happened and receiving only vague comprehension in return. It was probably this that terminated the brief attempt at romance, though I was fairly sure that her sister would have understood, and laughed with or at me.

I only discovered afterwards that this was the sister of the girl I had actually asked out, and this was the last time I went out with either of them.

Although they had their revenge when the girls' hockey team wanted a practice session against a men's side made up of members of the club. On at least three occasions, they chopped at my ankles with their sticks, rather than the ball, as I endeavoured to run past them.

One of these slashes resulted in a hairline fracture to my ankle, as I discovered after having an x-ray. It was very uncomfortable when I went underground, but I just continued to work as normal.

After my turn going out with one of them, I discovered that there were several people I knew, who had shared the same short-term fate as me.

At least there was always the compensation of a nearby general store where I could buy alcohol and biltong; something that I grew to love despite it hanging from string attached to the ceiling in the shop was usually covered in flies.

Recounting the dance story, I was somehow reminded of another day and another odd and comical experience. This was one winter's evening, and it was dark, except for a few street lights, when I had gone out for a stroll for some reason, towards the railway line and industrial area when I noticed smoke coming from a small factory building in the near distance. Then I heard the clang of a bell on a small fire engine, with a couple of ladders on top coming past me, with some of the crew standing and hanging on to its outside.

The fire engine looked to me like something from pictures I had seen of appliances used before and during the war and in black-and-white silent movies. Anyway, all they had was a (to me), tiny little vehicle pulling a pump of nearly the same size with a coil of hoses on top, to later connect to a fire hydrant.

When I got there, I could see the factory building alight, with flames licking at the front windows, and a lorry and a few cars parked next to it at the back, near what was probably a pull-down delivery entrance. What I couldn't see, and didn't know then, was that this was a candle manufacturer. It seemed a bizarre business to be in the middle of the Orange Free State, but odd things can go on, certainly around here.

From what I could see of the firemen, they seemed totally unprepared for this kind of emergency, as probably they usually only had to deal with fires when a braai, or barbcue, got out of hand. I had certainly never heard of a major fire locally.

Apparently, the firemen were unable to get into the building but had managed to smash a couple of windows above them at the front, through which they were spraying water, with the help of a couple of metal ladders against the wall.

They obviously had no idea what the factory contained as they seemed to be quite content to concentrate on where they were, but out under the shuttered roller door at the other end, lit candle wax was flowing towards the half dozen vehicles parked nearby.

I watched, amazed at the apparent lack of concern by the fire crew, as the burning candle wax flowed slowly towards, and then under a car that itself caught fire. It was only then that the handful of firemen ran to try and tackle this new outbreak, with just a couple of fire extinguishers in their hands.

Somehow, they managed to move a lorry parked next to the car that itself was in danger of catching alight as the burning wax had already reached it.

I stayed for about twenty minutes longer to observe the goings on that seemed more and more incompetent as time went on, and could only walk away shaking my head and laughing at Welkom's version of the Keystone Cops.

Something that was very strange but not so funny was the annual fitness test for every white employee in the mines that came up a couple of weeks later.

The assessment was undertaken by doctors, or so we were told, on an upper floor of the medical centre. The rooms they used could only be reached by two flights of stairs that went around the inside of the square, white-painted entrance hall.

Each time I went there, I saw in front of me at least one or two miners in their forties or fifties, coughing, occasionally stopping and hanging on to the bannisters, and then struggling to pull themselves up the last few steps to reach their destination.

Not everyone was from President Steyn, but I knew a couple of them and was later surprised to find them still working underground. Apparently, they had been passed by the doctors as being perfectly fit—A1 one of them later told me as he chatted with me after I had finished work in his stope.

For some reason, I also remembered that about this time, one of the scariest things that happened to me was my lamp going out suddenly when I was on my own. This was the second time it had happened, but on the previous occasion, I had just entered a worked-out stope, and there was still a little crack of light from the crosscut for me to see and head for.

This time I was also using another worked-out stope as a travelling way to the level below where I knew I might be able to catch an early cage to the surface, leaving my crew to catch the normal twelve o'clock cage, as they would not have been allowed to travel with me.

All was well until I had travelled about a hundred feet or so down the disused raise and fortunately just passed an open boxhole when, suddenly, my light failed. No, hitting the lamp or the battery on my back did any good, and I was in pitch blackness.

I wondered about going back up but could not remember the exact reverse of my journey thus far, and as I had used this travelling way a couple of times before, I thought the risk was less as my semi-photographic memory would help me. So I continued on down.

The only real dangers were the two more unguarded boxholes in the raise below me.

I also remembered that there were no loose rocks or rusty cables in the way. Nevertheless, with no light at all I would have to tread carefully and simply follow the route down.

I used one hand to follow the hangwall so that I knew I was going downhill, while my right arm waved about in front of me and also to the right, so I could touch the piled-high pit props next to me, except for the gaps between them of course.

Unfortunately, it was hard to judge exactly where I was, so I also used my right foot to kick at the footwall as I passed each prop. The reason for this was that if there was no contact, I would have reached an ATC that was normally cut deeper than the rest of the footwall to allow rock from the face to be winched to a boxhole.

It also meant that I knew a boxhole was near at hand, so the sensible thing was to step into the ATC and, with my back to the pit prop, edge forward to the one below before edging around this new one. Thus, hopefully, avoiding a quick exit to the level below, if the boxhole was where I thought it should be.

Having gone a few props further, I decided to swap sides and go down the left or west side, as I remembered that, at the level below me, instead of a bottom pit prop, it was missing to allow easier ingress and egress to the exit.

I also knew that the bottom boxhole came out slightly above the low side of the bottom ATC and was wider than normal. It was also unguarded. The footwall, where the wider exit was, had also been cut away to avoid people tripping.

All I had to do, when I reached this gap, was walk gingerly left to the face, then turn right and follow the face down a few yards until I reached the corner and I could turn left into the crosscut, again hugging the left wall until I could see faint light under the crosscut airlock doors.

Then I was able to heave a sigh of relief, find my way to open the doors and make my way to the well-lit haulage and back to the station.

About a year after arriving in Welkom, a new face appeared and got into the group of us who regularly met and played cards, or were involved with the same sports as me.

I don't know why, but a couple of weeks after we got to know him, he asked if a couple of us would like to try water skiing. Before this offer, I had wondered who had brought along a speed boat that was parked in one of the car parking bays at the back of the hostel.

I jumped at the chance to do something different, and three of us got into his car one Sunday to go to one of the local pans (or lakes). I don't know why or how they exist, but they are only about six to ten feet deep, so not too much of a concern if, like me, you're a poor swimmer; particularly so, because the water is very salty and therefore quite buoyant.

Anyway, my turn was a bit of a disaster. After being pulled up onto my feet and feeling as though I was at least partially in control, my skis suddenly dipped forward, and I was thrown, cartwheeling forward into the lake.

Equally fortunate was the realisation afterwards that I was immediately floating on the water with my skis sticking up in the air in front of me, and not trying to drown underneath. This was because of the high level of salt in the pan, rather like in the Dead Sea.

We only got one turn each, and then our benefactor decided that even though the other two managed better than me, the fun for him of driving his speed boat about was over, and we trailed back home.

However, on the return journey, we passed another pan. This one was just about covered by the almost homogenous pink of flamingos standing in the water. It was the only time I'd seen them in the wild, and it was a wonderful sight, particularly in the normally quite bland countryside around Welkom.

I had turned twenty and decided that during the week after cricket finished, I would take a skiing holiday in Austria and visit my mum and friends in Kent for the rest of the time.

My flight from Welkom to another small aerodrome on the outskirts of Johannesburg was leaving around lunchtime, and I booked a couple of taxis to both get me to the local airstrip and then another from the small airport outside Johannesburg, where we had to land, to take me to Jan Smuts, for the international flight.

When I boarded the Dakota, there was only one other person in the cabin, and he was sitting right at the front, and I was sitting near the back, a bit behind and looking out over the starboard wing.

I don't remember seeing any notice about seat belts, but apparently, that didn't matter when we took off. There was no communication from the pilot and no cabin crew to tell us what to do. I had flown in a Dakota before in England to take a holiday in Guernsey so knew it was very robust, or so I was told then.

Anyway, the flight was fairly normal until we neared the Vaal River. Then, above it, I could see a wall of dark, menacing clouds of what turned out to be thunderstorms spread out across the horizon as far as my eyes could see.

As we approached a river, we seemed to be turning to the West, and flying along it to see if there was a break in the clouds above.

After a short while, it seemed as though the pilot had given up on this course of action, as we suddenly turned sharply right and straight towards the clouds. Almost immediately the plane was lifted up and then dropped quite unexpectedly, and I was lifted out of my seat and hit my head on the luggage rack above.

At that point, I stopped trying to eat any more of the sandwiches I had brought with me and held on tightly to the arms of the seat. There weren't any seat belts that I could make out!

Looking out over the starboard wing, I could see heavy rain and lightning all around us. We were thrown up, down and sideways and occasionally there would be a jagged streak of lightning chasing through the rain and running over the wing.

This is a very sturdy aircraft, I told myself as I hung on for dear life, just hoping that the experience would soon end.

And then it did. Just as suddenly as we entered the cloud, we were back in full sunlight and going in to land. It was almost unbelievable that conditions could change just like this.

We came to a stop, and almost immediately, the door just behind me on my left opened, and I got down the stairs that had been parked there, walked over and took my bag from whoever had got it out of the hold, and then walked towards the large shed that operated as the terminal building. Before reaching it, a taxi drew up next to me and asked my name.

Having satisfied himself that I was his passenger, he took my case and put it in the boot as I settled into the front passenger seat, and then we shot off as fast as he could drive—it was a bit like being a navigator in a rally again, but at least these roads were wider than the country lanes we used in Kent.

The plane was late because of the storms, and an already tight schedule for the shortish trip to Jan Smuts but now getting there on time was almost impossible.

When at last we got to the airport, I grabbed my case and ran into the airport concourse but did not even reach the Lufthansa desk, before a lady in uniform rushed up to me and asked for my name. Then she grabbed my case and told me to run after her, unnecessarily informing me that I was late but that they had known I would be coming because the taxi company had let them know I was on my way.

There was no passport or other check, and I was whisked through a door onto the hard standing and ushered to the stairs at the front of the aircraft and was told to run up, while my case was being whisked away to be loaded.

The 707's engines were already going as I reached the top of the stairs and was ushered into the cabin.

Everyone looked at me as if I was some kind of celebrity, as I walked almost the length of the cabin to my seat.

The plane began to move, and I was told by a nearby stewardess to buckle up immediately.

Nothing much happened, apart from being served an evening meal, as we flew overnight towards Accra.

I had another window seat and could see the sea beneath us as we came in to land. There were also the lights shining off the ocean. Then, out of the dark, I made out what seemed like land, but it appeared to be moving slightly up and down. I guessed that it was mangroves, anyway, there were another series of lights.

Whether the pilot was confused by the two sets of lights, like me, the plane suddenly pulled up, and then the engines seemed to be pulled back, and we dropped quickly onto the runway, *bumping and travelling quite fast for a landing,* I thought.

Then I could clearly see the boundary fence coming unbelievably quickly towards us, and the plane turned immediately left, its right-wing tipping towards the ground. Then there was the diamond-shaped wired fence dashing past my window, a few feet from the wing.

The plane levelled out, and at last, we slowed to a more normal speed, and quite soon arrived at the terminal, with an opportunity to stretch our legs.

From Accra, we flew on to Frankfurt where we landed in a blizzard with no sight of land until only just being able to see a blackness of trees dashing past beside us as we were about to touch down on the runway.

Here I had to change planes from a 707 to a 727 for my onward flight to Heathrow.

This was without incident until I went to collect my baggage at Heathrow. I waited and waited but nothing. Then

I was joined by someone else. He was talking, or rather complaining, to a uniformed airport employee who was promising to forward his baggage, by taxi, to wherever he was going.

I heard the employee say, "Don't worry Mr Oppenheimer (the Chairman of Anglo-American Corporation and my distant boss!), I promise I'll do it myself." He also explained that our cases had been put in a different hold to the rest of the rest of the passengers, and that door had had to be unfrozen before it could be opened.

I was just about to ask for the same service when up popped our cases. The Heathrow employee got hold of Mr Oppenheimer's cases, put them on a trolley, and together they walked quickly away.

I picked up my mine, looked around and found my own way out—not the route the VIP took—into customs and immigration, then on to London by coach and underground, to catch a train down to Staplehurst, and my old home.

Mum had a bit of a shock when I knocked on the door and walked in—I hadn't warned her I was coming! After the shock, I remember her clasping me in her arms for a big hug.

But I was soon off again, the next day as it happens, this time heading back to London for my holiday in Westerndorf, Austria by coach, for a skiing holiday that I had booked back in Welkom.

When I arrived at the hotel (or hostel perhaps), I found out that I was sharing a room with three others – a bit of a surprise. But the place was warm, welcoming and generally comfortable.

It took a while to get a little bit of confidence going downhill, even after having some skiing lessons.

On the second day, a group of us learners were lined up down the slope for further instruction, when the seemingly common experience for such as ourselves occurred: someone reaching the bottom of the mountain ploughed straight into the trainee at the top, and we were all toppled, one after the other, like nine pins.

Anyway, just before going home, I did try using parallel skis, instead of the snowplough method, most of the way down from the top, except for a couple of tight corners when I needed to slow or risk careering into the pine trees.

Apres ski entertainment was all around, but my regular haunt was a disco where, unlike Welkom, there were plenty of girls to dance with but no one who seemed particularly special in my eyes although there was the odd kiss and cuddle.

Nothing particularly exciting happened during the rest of my stay in Staplehurst after I returned from skiing.

Mum was delighted to see me again and everyone I met seemed envious of my tan but nothing more though it was lovely seeing some of my old school friends, a couple of former girlfriends, as well as meeting the rest of my family.

It was a nice change but, apart from catching up on what had happened during the nearly year and a half that I'd been away, nothing out of the ordinary had occurred, other than I discovered that one of my close friends from school, and the girl I had been fairly serious about before leaving home, were now more or less an item.

However, the day before heading off again, I went back into Maidstone to say farewell to a couple of my friends who were still at school.

I also used some spare time to go into a record shop and asked if they had a copy of the Beatles' new album; Sergeant Pepper's Lonely Hearts Club Band.

The assistant told me, "Yes, but it's not on release until Friday." I asked if I could listen to a bit of it.

And, to my surprise, she said, "Yes," and told me to go and put some headphones on in a soundproof booth.

I immediately wanted to buy it, well knowing that it should not be sold yet. But, to my astonishment, when I showed her my airline ticket with my return date being the next day, she agreed. So I was able to play the record when I arrived back in Welkom the day before its official release date.

The flight back stopped at Nairobi airport, so I had a brief glimpse of what I guessed was Mount Kilimanjaro from my window seat.

When we landed, onward passengers were allowed to disembark to stretch their legs and look at the stalls of tourist goods on display in the transit lounge. Apart from tribal beads, most of the items were made from ivory. There were even some tusks among the carved items. I'm not sure that I was shocked, but there was something about their numbers that, apart from their price, made me feel that this was somehow wrong.

There was no more excitement on my way back to South Africa although I did enjoy the smoked salmon and caviar followed by a thick rump steak for dinner on the BOAC VC10, and even the Dakota and weather behaved themselves.

The return flight and skiing holiday had cost me almost half a year's average salary for people in England though it didn't seem that much to me.

Not very long after arriving back in Welkom, I finished very early one afternoon following doing some measuring and was lucky enough to see Mary-Anne waiting at the station when I arrived to go up top.

"I'm waiting to collect an injury," the bellman said when I reached it. "But there will be room for you if you want it."

I agreed as the main cages were being tested, and despite it being slow, I couldn't be bothered to wait another hour for one of them, but I did wonder how a stretcher could get into a space about five feet wide and three feet deep.

I would soon find out as the party of two arrived just after me and stood the stretcher upright, having strapped the injured black miner firmly onto it.

He was in terrible shape, and I wondered how he could be alive: the rim of his metal helmet was crushed into both sides of his head, making it a bit like a figure eight, and almost impossible to remove, and some of his bloody guts were protruding from bandages wrapped round his stomach. How the man survived the journey to the surface seemed a miracle to me. He made not a sound all the way up until he was returned to the horizontal, and then it was just a small kind of gurgle before he was rushed into a waiting ambulance. (I hope it was better than the one that later took me to hospital after breaking my leg.)

About a month later, I found out through my boss-boy that he had survived but was now hardly more than a vegetable. This was only possible because of my boss-boy's command of English. Most of the time I had to use the language called Fanakalo with the commonest phrases of 'up there', 'go there', 'come here', 'walk this way', 'walk quickly' or the like. Otherwise, just pointing was normally enough, as the team were well-trained and knew the English names of the things we used daily.

In many ways, this life was very quiet for a while.

I don't know why but the thought of the squashed head incident reminded me of going down six thousand feet one day and having to return to the surface immediately because I had such a pain in my head that grew worse and worse as we descended below forty level. It was like a sharp knife being forced between my eyes and feeling as though it was getting bigger and bigger to press and hurt my brain as we got ever lower.

Fortunately, there were only three stops on the way down and the pain almost subsided completely as we returned to the surface.

I changed and hurried back to the office and was immediately told by my boss to go and see my doctor. Luckily, someone else, from another part of the office block, was just getting into his car as I emerged from the offices, so I called out to ask if he was going into town, which he was.

When he realised why I was going, he diverted slightly to get me to see Dr Bolell once more.

Again he was quick to come to a diagnosis. He asked me to breathe through my nose so that he could see a pattern of microscopic water fogging up the cold mirror, as I breathed on it through my nose.

He showed me the result: one side was almost covered, while the other had hardly any mist at all. "One of your nostrils isn't working properly: it's almost closed. You need to have it seen at once. They'll just need to straighten the inside," he told me as he picked up the phone, rang and talked to someone about me, having confirmed my insurance status.

I learnt from his conversation that the soft part, the septal cartilage, was bowed in on my right side, and this was causing the problem in my sinuses and the consequent pain with a change of pressure.

Then he turned round to tell me, "I've booked an operation for you tomorrow." He told me the name of the hospital and its address—in Johannesburg!

I was astonished at the speed of this arrangement; a benefit of private medical insurance through my employer of course.

When I got back to the hostel I called my cousin as soon as I could. I had visited Mary and her husband when I had taken a couple of days holiday in Jo'burg some months earlier, and she had offered to put me up if I was in Jo'burg again.

She is a member of the Anglican persuasion as distinct from the Catholic relatives with whom I had had Christmas, but although their homes were not far apart, they never talked to each other. They were also much older, and I felt that I was a bit of a burden when I was there.

I asked if it would be possible to stay with her for a couple of days after I got out of the hospital, just in case something went wrong or if I needed to get back in quickly. Thankfully, they were kind enough to agree.

Now everything was arranged, I could pack some things and have a decent-sized meal before catching the overnight train to Jo'burg, where food would be off the menu until after my op.

I can't remember the exact events before I arrived at the hospital and had settled in to have the op that afternoon.

It was later explained that the skin or gristle in the middle of my nose had been cut out, and then turned round and put back to allow a better air passage.

This was a hot summer and there was just a sheet over me as it was so warm in the ward that I had been taken to after the operation, and I had woken up. I don't remember eating, either that night or in the morning after I woke up, again quite early, to see another bright, sunny day outside.

Before breakfast arrived at a more reasonable time, a nurse came in to remove my dressings.

She had brought a large bowl with her and sat down next to me and gently pulled the round, finger-width, white, but blood-soaked wadding from each nostril independently and let it drop, like a long dead worm, into the bowl.

The exercise went on for what seemed like ages, and almost completely filled the vessel.

Some blood was spilt on the sheet, so the nurse went out, took the bowl and, a short time later, returned with a new sheet, which she exchanged for the old one.

Having tucked it in, she set off for the door with the used one under her arm. As she got to the door, she turned towards me and started, "Whatever you do don't—"

"Aaaatishooo!"

"Sneeze."

Blood sprayed from my nose all over the new sheet and onto the floor.

At that moment, it looked as though she could quite happily kill me, "Oh, fff—ssshhh." Her eyes blazed with anger as she came to remove the mess on my bed and clean up the floor.

My weak 'sorry' was ignored, and she wouldn't look at me, but I could hear quiet chuntering coming from her, as she completed her task and went out again to get another clean sheet.

The replacement happened in stony, sullen silence. No words were exchanged, and I had no eye contact either. It was quite funny really, but she couldn't see the funny side of it. Although I certainly managed a bit of a chuckle after she left.

Only then did I realise that I was completely alone. The two others in the ward when I arrived yesterday were gone.

The surgeon arrived shortly after my breakfast, served by a different nurse, and gave me a brief examination, then told me that I could leave at noon, assuring me that I shouldn't bleed any more but to try not to blow my nose.

Another useless warning, I thought to myself, but fortunately, I didn't sneeze again for a long time.

I got a taxi to the Strick's house, where I enjoyed three days of recuperation, most of the time being out in their substantial garden, enjoying the early summer weather.

Mary was very kind, given that she also had a fairly new baby to look after (as I write, this baby is now a plastic surgeon in Glasgow) as well as her husband. It's terrible, but I can't remember his name; I do remember that he had quite an important job for a nearby local authority, Sandton, that he tried to explain to me.

It was nice to talk to someone I sort of knew for a change, but I didn't say much about my experiences underground, except to explain why I had needed the operation.

Then he asked if I played chess. As I used to be part of the team that played for my school, I jumped at the idea, so we amused ourselves playing until it was time for bed. We were fairly evenly matched, so the games were very enjoyable, particularly as there was nobody at Protea House who played.

Unfortunately, my brief 'holiday' was soon over, and I had to go back to Welkom to test out the efficacy of my reformed nose.

During my time as President Steyn, 4 Shaft was dug and developed, and I had a couple of very small parts in this.

The first event occurred at the time that it was only about fifty feet deep and had just the skeleton of the headgear built.

My job was to define the location of the exact centre of the top of one of the two upside-down vs with tops cut-off, to form horizontals, as arches for either side of the structure. In order to do this, I only needed my boss-boy to help carry my theodolite for me to do the task—also to be there if I fell off! Not that he would have been able to do much.

Getting to the top was frightening. Firstly, we had to climb a wooden ladder to about fifteen feet above the ground, then we had to cross over the gaping shaft on a horizontal girder, around one foot across and thirty or forty feet long, then transfer on to another similar girder to get to a point where we could climb the approximately three feet wide arm.

There were no safety features for this girder that was at an angle of around seventy degrees to the ground, when we had to climb to about a hundred and ten feet above the surface, with nothing to hang on to or use for the climb but the large rivets sticking up from the flat metal, like those you can see on the Tyne Bridge for example.

No one seemed to have heard of safety harnesses or handrails to hang on to them. We were just relying on our guts and apparent lack of fear to manage to get up and down.

Even when I arrived at the horizontal top, my ordeal was not finished. I had to set up the theodolite on its wooden box on the girder, ensure that my theodolite's base was horizontal and precisely aligned to the centre point of the twenty odd feet long structure at the top, and hope to keep the whole thing in place while observing and recording angles to three specific markers some distance away on the ground.

The first two sightings were comparatively easy: one was almost directly in front of me, where one side of the winding engine house would be, as the winding engines had to be exactly aligned with the winding wheels at the top of the headgear, and the other point at around fifty degrees to my left, which involved leaning round the theodolite to see it.

The third sighting was the scariest part of the whole operation, as I had to stride over the top of the theodolite in order to take the final reading, while not tripping over or moving the box in any way. Then, on my hands and knees once more, while missing more rivets, taking a sighting at about thirty degrees to the direction I had come up.

At least I was now using a lighter and more sophisticated machine than the one I had first had and destroyed, so the angles were displayed through the eyepiece for me. In this respect, it was a straightforward exercise. But I still had to hang on to my notebook and pencil, fearful of dropping either or both, which would have cost me a return journey as it was unlikely that, had they fallen into the shaft, I would be able to get them back as no one was down it, nor was the Mary-Anne operating that day.

Even holding on to the theodolite while my boss-boy opened its box lid, was not easy, balancing as I was on my knees on the flat iron girder.

Fortunately, this measuring task was completed early in the morning, well before the sun was at its hottest, and there was no wind to mention to make the whole enterprise more dangerous than it already was.

Climbing down after my ordeal was almost as bad, as I didn't want to look down to find my next footing, as we were going backwards down the girder, and I was afraid of losing my balance. However, I had to turn around sometimes to make sure I didn't bump into my boss-boy who was going first.

Fortunately, I was never asked to do such a stupid and dangerous thing again—I would never be able to be a steeplejack or build another Tyne Bridge. I still don't know how I managed to build up the guts to undertake this task either.

Apart from the actions I had to take, I have no other recollection of this job, except the extraordinarily strong feeling of relief when I was back on terra firma, but then I started shaking and had to sit down for a bit.

However, I was lucky in another respect, and that was because my boss-boy at the time spoke good English and had gained some GCEs back in Tanganyika, so communication was very easy, and we could pass the shaking time together by having a chat about his family.

Otherwise, most of the time underground I had to use Fanakalo: a made-up language combining tribal African and Afrikaans with the odd word of English.

One day, as we were close to finishing a job, and we had time to spare before getting the cage, I asked my boss-boy if he would like me to teach him how to do my job.

His reply was somewhat unexpected, "No Baas, I can't."

"Why can't you?"

"I come from the wrong tribe in Tanganyika, and if I said I could do this work, I would get into serious trouble."

So a kind of Apartheid existed there as well, I thought to myself, here because they are black and, in his country, because he would be getting above his station. What a strange world!

Whenever I could, I would try to talk to members of my little gang although I could only do that when no one else was around because, in this case, I would be in trouble if I did, and they might get a right telling off, or worse, for talking to me. Translation made these attempts a bit difficult as well.

However, I did learn a little about their different beliefs but even less about their lives.

Some of these beliefs I mixed up with the Christianity that I had been brought up on—even singing in the local church choir before my voice broke—so that I could cope a bit more easily with the possibility of being killed any day.

Perhaps this thought was strengthened by a bizarre evening when one of the groups I was with in Protea House proclaimed that he could hypnotise people. No one else put themselves forward, so muggins did.

I can't remember how his attempt started, but I was suddenly in a dream: I could picture myself in a sitting room in what could have been a fairly large house. The room had bay windows and thick heavy curtains hanging down, covering every window except the one on the left, where the light was streaming in onto the back of a girl's head that was silhouetted against the bright background. She appeared to be playing a black grand piano, though no noise accompanied this vision.

The hypnotist asked me what I could see, and I told the listeners that I was in a house in Wales, as well as the sight above.

How I should know that it was in Wales I have no idea.

My hypnotist took me out of my trance, and this was when the group told me what I had said about what I could see, and as they did so, the picture came back into my mind. I have retained this image until today.

Which year this event occurred, I can't remember, but it was yet another when I was lucky more than once.

I had been instructed to go down with a shift boss to an old, worked-out stope, next to another, where the chief surveyor thought a whole section of rock, called a pillar, had not been mined out at the time of its closure.

If it was true, it would be important to mine it out as the reef here was of very high value.

The time of going down had been set at nine o'clock, much later than normal, so it was a leisurely trip to the shaft that morning.

After I changed and got my lamp, I went to wait at the shaft top along with mine and the shift boss's boss-boy. The bellman was by the cage, regularly looking at his watch.

Suddenly, the shift boss appeared, running around the corner of a nearby building.

"I'm sorry I'm a bit late, but I was in the middle of an argument with the winding-engine driver."

The bell rang, and we were quickly ushered into the cage by the bellman.

Very unusually, black and white were in the same deck, just because it would be easier for the bellman.

Down we went at normal speed until we got to thirty-eight level when, unusually, the cage hardly slowed. Perhaps the driver is trying to catch up with his schedule, I wondered to myself as we continued down past forty-eight at a speed greater than normal. There was no sign of slowing as we approached fifty or five thousand feet down, where we were supposed to get off. Instead, just as we saw the light from it come into view, the cage accelerated momentarily, and we felt the effect of the emergency brakes going on within the winding engine itself.

This only allowed the cable holding the cage to stretch further on down to five-two then the station lights at five thousand four hundred feet came into view.

We went past it a little way, then yo-yoed back up, well past forty-eight level when again we started to descend. At this point, a strange smell emanated from the shift boss's boss-boy, but that didn't stop us. Down another four hundred feet and then up again until, at last, we stopped, amazingly, precisely at fifty level, much to our relief, although I think the boss-boy was relieved much earlier!

After we left the cage and had walked a little, the boss-boy was allowed a short break to dive into a white-walled toilet, carved out from the haulage side wall, and then walked slowly on for him to catch us up near the crosscut we needed to use.

All the while I tried to imagine how a cable of twisted metal, at least five centimetres in diameter, could stretch so far and yet finish at the right depth.

My mind changed back to the job in hand as we entered the stope we wanted, and walked upright to the top of the raise. This was another stope where all the shale had been removed, so I thought it would be quite easy to get to the pillar that was supposed to be on our left, and about a third of the way down the stope.

However, the miner had left unusually large gaps between the high, squared-off pillars and single round poles that propped up the hangwall, and as a consequence, both forms of resistance were squashed, the poles looking a bit like brown palm trees where the hangwall had simply bent, but much of the rest of the roof had collapsed between us and the face we needed to look at, so the pillar, if it was there, could not be seen from the raise.

We went into the ATC below where the pillar was supposed to be, but much of the hangwall had collapsed as we approached where we thought the old face should be, leaving a fairly narrow path to the face. Where it narrowed, we could look up and see large chunks of rock above us that seemed to be suspended in mid-air, as there were cracks all around their bases as far as I could see.

No matter how hard I looked, there was nothing at all holding them in place it seemed. Ignoring this potential danger, as was quite normal, we moved on past and under the unusual pattern of rocks above the face itself.

We thought that the pillar would be very noticeable, as the stope we were in had had all the shale removed above the reef, so the face should have been more or less a quite high wall of rock if it was there, but there was no way to see it. It didn't matter whether we tried looking lower, after our first attempt going up the slope was stopped by an old rock fall, as even more of the roof had collapsed there, too, now preventing us from going down as well as up.

So back to the front of the ATC. Here we could see through a narrow, horizontal gap to the neighbouring stope that had also been worked out. The gap was narrow because it had been mined out normally, with the shale still above. But it, too, had come down perhaps a foot or two, while our footwall had remained about four inches below where the reef had been.

We took a short break for a drink before setting off to leave the stope, no pillar having been found.

Having finished our brief interlude, there was the noise of a large rockfall somewhere nearby. Dust from the fall rushed along the ATC towards us. It didn't take long to clear, so we ventured back towards the raise, only to see the way completely blocked by large slabs of rock at least fifteen feet high, leaving a ragged kind of saucer-shaped rock formation above them.

Sure enough, it was where we had passed the suspended rocks as we had walked in.

None of us volunteered to try and get over it, as it was impossible to know how stable it, or the rest of the hangwall above, was.

So back to the front of the ATC to see if the gap to the next stop was big enough for us to squeeze through—it wasn't!

Then we spread out because, although we could see into the worked-out stope, there was only a narrow gap of two to five inches between our footwall and the hangwall of the older stope that had been mined normally.

The only way of escape would have to be through the neighbouring worked-out stope. Any idea of a search for the pillar had long gone.

In the meantime, a search by our bossboys, further down below the ATC, found nothing but more fallen rock, thus making escape that way impossible too.

So, once again, in pairs, we searched up and down for a gap wide enough to get through.

It was the shift boss going down the stope who found the only possibility, so I went down to it with the others to join in the attempt, after he had shouted up to us.

It was fortunate that we were all quite slim because we only just managed to wriggle through the narrow gap that the shift boss had already entered.

But, even then, our problems were not over because the hangwall in this old, normally mined stope had sagged for as far as we could see from the face, and it was by no means certain whether we could get out this way either, even though the footwall in this stope was lower than that we left behind.

The shift boss and I had a brief chat about whether to wait for rescue, but it would be at least two and a half hours before the alarm was raised. And then it might be some time before anyone got near, so we decided to try to find a way through this old stope. If there was a direct route, it would only be about four or five hundred feet to the upper crosscut, but the way was by no means simple.

Nevertheless, off we went, the shift boss first and me following in the rear.

Soon the hangwall was so low that I had to remove my hard hat to get through this section of the stope. Even with my head on its side, the rim of the hard hat jutted out too far to allow egress.

I began to wonder if we would ever get out, and the Beatle's song 'Help' came into mind as we squirmed along;

"Help me if you can I'm feeling down, And I do appreciate you being round, Help me get my feet back on the ground, Won't you please, please help me?" over and over again, as we twisted and turned, went around in circles sometimes but eventually found a gap between footwall and hangwall widening enough for us to more than wriggle, until eventually we reached the old raise, and could stand with a bit of a stoop to go up it to the crosscut.

At least the ventilation doors in it were not tight shut, like they should have been to stop air getting in or out of this worked-out section, and we were able to push them against the outside pressure from the haulage.

Our ordeal had taken so long that we only just made the cage to the surface.

How wonderful it was to smell the fresh air and see the sun shining as the shutter door was opened.

There was a slight pause as the bellman opened the gate and let the fairly crowded cage gradually empty, with me being the last to leave.

I put my left foot onto the solid, sunny concrete. Then, just as my back foot left the cage's floor, there was an almighty crack and the cage suddenly dropped down the shaft behind me, as the cable above parted company with the cage, swinging back wildly towards the winding engine house.

Luckily, the cage just managed to miss my heel as it picked up speed and dropped past my back.

My lucky day, or what?

Later, I discovered that the winding engine driver, who had had that argument with the shift boss earlier, had been killed when the cable broke and whipped back, braking through the winding engine's roof.

When, in July 1969, more than a year after my climb of the headgear, I switched on the radio to listen to the moon landing, I also put on my tape recorder and played the Rolling Stones singing *2000 Light Years From Home* and managed to record Neil Armstrong's words: "That's one small step for man. One giant leap for mankind," over the top.

The next day, I told my (Tom's old) gang that there was a man walking on the moon, and they just laughed. "You're kidding us baas, there couldn't be," they responded.

It was hardly surprising because many of the black workers were still very tribal. Indeed there was an annual ritual in the mine about Easter time each year, when members of one tribe, I think it was Xhosas, used to catch a Basotho, cut his chest open and eat his still beating heart.

I wondered why there was no police action after this murder had taken place. But I was told that this was a tribal thing, and as such, it was not a matter for the police. Apparently, black people could do whatever they liked among themselves if it was a tribal matter.

It wasn't very important if one black man, or more, killed another black, or stole something, again from a black person. These matters would normally be settled by tribal elders, but in the mines, no such arrangements had been made, so nothing happened.

Only if a black man did something against a white person would the police be involved.

Not long after this, it turned out to be the last year that I would hear about the ritual as I left mining for good.

Shortly before my climb up the headgear, there was another climb that I had undertaken.

Following a game of cricket on our home ground, some of the team and a couple of wives were chatting and having a few drinks, when one couple I started talking to decided to go home.

They asked each other if they had their flat keys, and neither had. Apart from telling each other off for not bringing a set, they started discussing how they could possibly get in.

At this point, I asked if they had an open window, and they had, so I volunteered to try to climb in if I could.

They took up my offer and promised to get me home afterwards whatever the outcome because, at this time, I hadn't passed a driving test.

When we arrived outside their block of flats I saw the top their bathroom window on the first floor was open, so this was an obvious but difficult place to get in.

In order to do this, I first had to climb up a waste pipe, also servicing a neighbouring flat, then go along the connection that led to their toilet where it went through the wall. At this point, the bathroom wall was set back and had a purely decorative brick archway in front. Unfortunately or fortunately, that left a small gap to step over to get onto the bridge of bricks, itself about a foot away from the inset bathroom wall and the small open window above a narrow fixed one, with a narrow sloping ledge below that was about three feet up from the archway.

So I was just able to stretch up to hold on to the bottom of the open window's frame and shift my feet onto the narrow ledge below it.

From there I somehow managed to get my head, shoulders and arms through the narrow hole and by wriggling somewhat uncomfortably over the sticking-up piece of metal of the window's catch, I found myself head down with my hands on the top of the toilet cistern. It felt a bit slippery, so I quickly got my hands on the open toilet seat, with my hips trying to make it through the window, and my legs flailing around outside trying to edge my hips forward in order to get the rest of my body in.

They succeeded with a suddenness that surprised me and found me all at once in a heap on the floor, luckily missing the bowl's edge and not breaking my neck by diverting into it.

I got myself up and gave myself a quick check to see if everything was still okay, then made my way to the bathroom door and quickly thereafter to their front door—the whole being an act that I would not wish to repeat if I could avoid it. Only the Dutch courage from alcohol enabled me to undertake the task this time.

I can't remember exactly when I got a provisional licence, bought a mini and started to learn to drive with help from drivers in Protea House.

Another, to me more interesting chat with a colleague's wife earlier in the year, ended with her offering to read my hand to tell me my future. She said that in the near future, I would be going on a long journey, *a typical line,* I thought, as I couldn't imagine my doing that for years to come, except for a holiday back in the UK. She then told me that about four years later I was going to be very ill.

I saw her looking very carefully at my hand and frowning as she said this, and then she added, "You're going to be in hospital for a long time."

How could she possibly know that in 1974, I would be working in Charing Cross Hospital for four years? I almost stopped listening after this. Certainly, her further prediction about the number of children I would have was later proved wrong.

Two weeks after the prediction, I was sitting beside her, waiting for my turn to bat, when there was a feeling that the ground was moving. It seemed to be in her direction, so I looked, and to my surprise, a small hole around two feet wide had appeared beneath her deck chair.

Naturally, I got up, told her what I could see and asked her to move, so I could look down the hole. It was disappointingly not very deep, about six feet I guessed, but there was no rhyme or reason for a hole like that to appear on the surface.

As everyone on our side was engaged in mining in one way or another, no one else could suggest a reason for it either.

She obviously could not read her own hand as she probably would not have sat there if she had.

The hole remained but was ignored for as long as I worked in the mine at least.

A few weeks later I was doing, for me, something else unexpected, but this time going down not up: I was asked to assist a colleague to make checks on the downward progress of Four Shaft's ventilation shaft.

Travelling down was a bit different to the usual trip in a cage: in order to do, so we had to climb into a very large bucket, around eighteen feet in diameter, with walls about four feet high and a couple of inches thick.

It was quite slow, and the bucket swayed slightly without hitting the sides, which were less than two feet away.

Nearing the bottom, we needed to check some measurements to ensure that the girders, fitted to the sides, were vertical and the right distance apart. We edged gradually downward to repeat the checks about four times.

Eventually, we stopped just above the bottom, and a ladder was put up the side of the shaft for the miner to get onto, to check that the charges were in place and ready to go. Then he and his two bossboys got in, and we all started on up again.

I failed to notice at the time that the miner had brought a plunger on board and therefore was somewhat surprised when, about forty feet off the bottom, the explosives went off, wobbling the bucket and surrounding us in noise, smoke and the smell of cordite, which seemed to stick around us almost until the surface.

I had wondered why he had brought a coil of rope with him and now realised that he needed to lower the now obsolete plunger back to the bottom of the shaft in order to use it again for the next blast.

I was quite pleased to avoid any future trips of this kind.

However, something similar to this happened one day about a year later, when I was asked to check the progress of a return airway.

Me and my boys went down the now functioning Four Shaft where new haulages were being developed. Our task was to go into a return airway and put in a couple of pegs so as to accurately direct the tunnel over the top of established haulage.

Firstly, we needed to find the miner to report our presence, but he was nowhere to be seen. His box, just inside the temporary entrance to the airway, was locked up and there was no sound of drilling. Just in case, I walked further along the haulage to where there was an entry point to the airway on the other side. There was no sound of movement or activity there, either. So I assumed that he wasn't working today for some reason. I did not know that sometimes these miners could be working on a second development in a completely different location, and I had no means of knowing if that was the case.

Anyway, we went into the initial entry and successfully added the first peg close to where the tunnel had started to flatten out over the top of the haulage. Now I had to put in another peg close to the face; so that the miner could be sure that he would be at the right height and direction to not cause this tunnel to break into the haulage below it, and to meet the airway at the other side, also at the right point.

Having secured bobs hanging down from the pegs at the right heights for the miner to be able to line them up, and identify the tunnel's centre to keep it horizontal. My boss-boy and I were just packing up our things when a muffled series of bangs went off fairly close to us, the explosions being powerful enough for small pieces of rock to fly past us at some speed fortunately.

I remember shouting, "What the hell?" and suggesting that we got out quickly.

Emerging into the haulage once more, there was the miner coming towards us.

He was obviously a bit concerned when he realised that we had been on the receiving end. He apologised and explained to me that he had indeed been working elsewhere when we arrived.

He had not noticed us at the time when he had gone into the other side of the return airway to set off the charges, thinking it would be well before our arrival.

"I'm so glad that no one got hurt," he said shakily.

I quickly showed him what we'd done; he apologised again, and then we set off for the station. It was just an ordinary sort of day really—nothing remarkable to tell anyone else about.

I can't remember exactly when I got a provisional licence, bought a mini and started to learn to drive with help from my qualified driver friends in Protea House but must have been around the New Year that I started taking driving lessons and practised some more with them.

One Saturday a few weeks later, I was in my room in Protea House, when one of the waiters from the restaurant knocked on the door to tell me that I was wanted on the phone. This was very odd, as I knew nobody who would ring the public phone, let alone the one in the manager's office.

I made my way around and picked up the phone and said, "Hello," in a curious sort of way.

"Happy twenty-first birthday," was the response.

Of all people, I heard my brother in England speaking to me. I couldn't believe it.

How had he got this number? I hadn't passed it on to anyone because I didn't know it myself. Anyway, because of the cost then, the call was only a couple of minutes long.

I had no time to tell of my lucky escapes, as three minutes or so of the call seemed to disappear so quickly.

About a month later I had been looking forward to another holiday skiing in Austria, and I was due to fly from Johannesburg the next Saturday.

This was the last week of league cricket, and to be sure to win the league, we had to finish the last match with a win. We just had to bowl our opponents out, so everyone was keen on the field as a draw might not be enough.

A ball was hit, not very hard but past me, into the outfield. I raced back from my silly mid-on position and managed to bend down, scoop up the ball and throw it to the stumps behind me, and just past my ankles, all in one go.

I didn't see the outcome because, running in from the boundary, was another, much heavier fielder than me. Unfortunately, in his haste to also get the ball, he tripped over a clump of grass and his shin, came down on my outstretched leg.

A sharp crack and I was prone on the ground.

He lifted me up as though to attention. "You'll be alright," he said as my right leg steadied itself, but now with a new articulated knee halfway down my shin, that had allowed my foot more leeway than usual so that, instead of being next to my left foot, it was nearly six inches away with only the inside edge of the sole on the ground.

"Then, perhaps not," he said as he lowered me once more onto the ground, my right leg now being somewhat contorted. Other players had rushed up, keen to get on with the game, and me off the field of play.

Quickly, one pulled my feet together and slipped two fingers, one each into the bottom of my trouser legs, and with someone else holding my shoulders, they lifted me horizontally from the ground and hurried towards the boundary.

Unfortunately, one of the fingers of the leg carrier slipped its hold and the end of my right leg was once again free

120

to move, this time to the vertical, so I had a second knee. It was soon gathered up, and with even more haste and less ceremony, I was dumped just off the field of play, with the boundary line right by next to my left arm.

As I waited for someone to appear or something to happen, all I could do was watch as my right foot slowly moved on its own, until it lay horizontal on the ground, leaving my left foot stark upright; the sign of a learner walker.

What surprised me, about all that had happened thus far, was that I experienced no pain at all despite both tibia and fibula being broken. I lay there for some time just thinking about whether I would get my money back for the skiing holiday in Austria that I was due to take the next Saturday until an ambulance mysteriously arrived at my side.

To call it an ambulance was a bit of an exaggeration. Actually, it was a standard van with a ridged metal floor. Only it being white with a red cross and the word 'ambulance', painted on the sides told me what it was supposed to be.

At some point, I was offered morphine, but the ambulance driver remembered that he had forgotten to put any in the van that morning, so I went without, not that I needed it. They did at least strap my legs and feet together before putting me onto a canvas stretcher, and then a thick blanket on the metal floor of the van for some protection from banging my head and body on it during my ride to the hospital.

However, I remember little of the journey, but I do recall being checked to see if I had medical insurance; otherwise, they would not have been able to take me in for treatment at that hospital.

After this, the next I remember is waking up in bed with a plaster cast from my foot to the very top of my leg.

Initially, it was trouble to sit up and eat or drink anything, but very soon, I was out of bed and sitting with difficulty, and somewhat precariously, on the front of a chair. I don't remember how I managed to go to the toilet on my bed during the first couple of days, but I do remember getting to know one of the nurses rather well—perhaps it was, at least in part, an unconscious signal I gave her through the sheet covering whenever she came into the ward.

After a couple of days, she asked if I would like her to visit me at visiting time in the evening. She was quite attractive, so of course I agreed.

As I had been equipped with a pair of crutches I was better able to move around, and they were a perfect fit in a toilet cubicle to be made into a cross so that I could rest my leg on them. It was very much better than the other situation when I had to sit more or less on the edge of the seat because the height of the top of the cast made any other position all but impossible.

I also received a bouquet of flowers from the chairman of the cricket league, which was a bit of a surprise, but regular visits from my nurse were not, and I enjoyed sitting out on the balcony outside the ward with her.

Anyway, when I was soon to be discharged, another patient, who was in his early twenties and had broken his left leg in seven places during a motorbike accident, was moved from another ward into a bed near mine.

His nurse friend and mine were on nights one day and either a visitor friend of his or the nurse from the other ward, who had taken an immediate shine to him when he had been brought in, had brought a bottle of brandy into the ward. So, just after the last round, sometimes a little after midnight, we all assembled on the other side of our ward, where there was a small table, for a little party.

An hour or so later, the nurses needed to do another round, so it was time for us to go to bed. The motorcyclist began showing off in front of his girlfriend by racing away to his bed on his crutches.

As he got to his bedside, near the head of the bed, he swung his legs back, and as they swung forwards, he managed to turn his legs sideways to launch himself, feet first, onto the high hospital bed. He obviously miscalculated this new manoeuvre as, instead of staying on top, the weight of his cast took him further than planned, and he disappeared over the far side of the bed, landing on his right side, his thigh-high plaster cast covering his left leg landing heavily on his pristine right one, breaking it as well.

My nurse quickly helped me back into my bed and then went to help her colleague with her boyfriend.

The brandy must have had its effect fairly quickly, as I was soon asleep, so I don't know what happened and when. But when I woke later in the morning, the motorcyclist was back in his bed, now with both his legs in plaster.

How this incident was explained I know not because I was discharged soon after breakfast and I didn't see either him or his nurse again. But it must be unusual for a patient to arrive with one broken leg and leave the hospital with two.

I can't remember cancelling the holiday I had planned or how it was done, but I do have this warning: be careful what you do before you go skiing.

I got a taxi back to the hostel and then found how difficult it was to get around: having a meal in the restaurant, using the toilet, washing and climbing up and down stairs could be a bit of a struggle. For one thing, my right leg was straight as a dye from my groin downwards, it was heavy, and at first, I was not allowed to put weight on it. So what do you do with it going upstairs?

Pushing your leg out in front of you is impossible because the next step up is in the way, and trying to leave it behind, as it were, only made you fall backwards if you were foolish enough to try it. So the only other thing to do was a long-winded hop sideways—not easy when you have crutches under your armpits and can't hold on to the bannisters, but somehow I managed it without having an accident.

My nurse girlfriend visited me a couple of times after I was discharged. We seemed to be getting on very well, but having my leg in plaster made the occasions a bit restricted, and any serious form of intimacy was nigh impossible.

The third time she asked if she could borrow a few of my single records asking, as she was leaving, if I would like to come with her to visit her home on Saturday.

She told me to be ready for ten o'clock when she would come in a car to give me a lift.

I agreed and was in the waiting area with a packed suitcase at the appointed time.

I waited and waited, watching the comings and goings of other residents.

Eventually, after waiting for about an hour, I rang the nurse's home only to be told that she had left more than an hour earlier. I was never to see or hear from her again, or to get my records back. Probably, there was a fitter fella who had come into the ward after me.

Apart from being very annoyed at being let down, she had taken my favourite singles.

One Sunday night, while still in plaster, I was playing bridge with three friends in the hostel, and when we had finished, we all felt a bit hungry. One of our numbers went off to see if the restaurant kitchen was open. It wasn't, so everyone agreed to go into town to see if anywhere was still open at this time; a little after eleven o'clock. So we headed downstairs from the room we had been playing in and got into one member's car to look around the likely places. I was wedged into the front passenger's seat, along with my crutches.

All were shut, so someone in the back seat said that he knew a place, a garage, that he said was open all night and had food and drink in machines.

Apparently, it was just outside Bethlehem. I hadn't heard of it before, but it didn't matter to me as I wasn't back working at that time. Anyway, the name sounded promising, and we sct off.

At around two o'clock, we pulled into the garage forecourt where we could see the machines under lights.

We agreed on what we would be happy with, and a couple of the group got out and went to the machines. I could see them walk over to talk to the petrol attendant and could see him shaking his head.

They returned empty-handed but asked if either of the remaining passengers had any five-cent pieces for a coffee, as only exact money could be used.

I managed to find one in my pocket, the only one among us. So this was taken and one cup was brought over for us all to share.

A round trip of about two hundred and twenty miles, arriving back home at a little after four o'clock, all for a quarter of a cup of coffee and a sighting of a shooting star. Yet another mad thing that happened to me.

As time went by, my broken leg became more and more itchy, and I had to use a ruler, or anything else slim and hard, to scratch it as near to my ankle as I could, but I couldn't get below my knee, so the itchiness in my lower leg got progressively worse.

Eventually, after eleven weeks in plaster, I went back to the hospital to have my plaster removed and my leg checked.

When it came out of plaster, it was an even more horrible, skinny, smelly sight than I hoped it would be, and I wanted to disown it, but that was impossible without losing it completely.

Fortunately, I had remembered to bring the other slip-on shoe and a matching sock with me, and managed to walk back to the hostel, though rather shakily and feeling intensely embarrassed when anyone looked at me.

When I knew that my plaster was soon to be removed, I managed to write to my aunt in Cape Town to see if it would be alright to visit her for a couple of days, starting the next weekend following the cast's removal. (I had holidays to take any holidays that had to be finished by a week later.)

Anyway, I received a letter back almost immediately and fortunately managed to book a driving test for after work on Friday.

My leg felt a bit strange as if disconnected in some way, and my foot sometimes seemed to move sideways as I drove. I warned the examiner that my leg had just come out of plaster, but he simply ignored my admission and got on with the test.

All went surprisingly well, given the short space of time that I had to practice again.

The oral test of the Highway Code was easy enough, and the practical test of manoeuvring, parking and hill starting on the purpose-built track went quite well.

I was quite surprised by the hill start because the land around Welkom is quite flat.

Anyway, I passed that and was then commanded to go out on the open road. This part was less easy, as my brain kept thinking that the lower part of my leg was semi-detached, and I couldn't be sure what my foot was doing. Again I managed to pass this part of the test as well, so I knew that I could leave on my seven-hundred-mile journey the next day.

I just managed to throw a few things together to put in my suitcase, have breakfast and set off around seven in the morning for my twelve-hour journey. I had already bought insurance for when I passed my test.

Apart from stopping to fill up with petrol, and a couple of short stops to get something to eat, I drove steadily but as fast as I could to Bloemfontein and then on the road to Cape Town.

Most of the journey seemed fairly flat, with scrawny bushes in the sandy surrounds, but as evening was coming, I started to drive through some mountains, still travelling at between sixty and seventy in my mini.

There were two steep hills close together just after I turned a bend, and between them what appeared to be a deep valley. I didn't get a good look because a sudden gust of wind blew me onto the rough dirt to the side of the road. Then, as I tried to get the car back onto the tarmac, another strong gust blew me over the edge of the road, the car rolling three or four times down a fairly steep bank, before settling on its wheels, about twenty feet from what looked like a dry river bed.

The roof was twisted sideways, as was the offside rear wheel. Of course, all the glass was shattered, but otherwise, both I and the car were in one piece; I could even open my side door. I just had a small scratch above my forehead and another on a finger but was otherwise unscathed.

I was quite amazed as then there were no seatbelts. So too were the three drivers who had seen what happened and rushed down the road to see if they could help, probably expecting a far worse sight.

One offered me a lift and also suggested that I might be able to drive my car to a garage that might be able to carry out the repairs and that it was not far away, and then he would take me from there to Cape Town.

So I did as suggested and amazingly managed to somehow get my car up the bank and onto the road and about seven miles to the garage, where I left the car and the details of my insurer.

It was a good job I had passed my test the day before—my insurance was now valid!

Remarkably, my good Samaritan driver was going to his home which happened to be in the road parallel to my aunt's in Newlands, so he took me to her door. How lucky can you get?

Of course, I saw my relatives, including my cousin, Lorna, who was born around the same time I was, and with whom I exchanged Christmas cards and a written note each year until I was in my teens.

I also went up Table Mountain and round to the point to see the baboons. From here I could see a wavy line in the ocean where the Atlantic and Indian Oceans met, but other trips were not possible without my car. I also needed to find a way back to Welkom as cheaply as possible.

So I looked in the newspapers, where people sometimes advertised for someone who could drive to accompany them to Johannesburg, as well as some other locations, but not Welkom. So I was lucky enough to get one, sharing some of the driving of a Mercedes, to Jo'burg and then caught an overnight train down to Welkom. But that meant me leaving my aunt's earlier than I had intended.

Returning to Protea House meant that I was now in full harness to return to my work underground again. Also, I was surprised that it was only a couple of weeks until my car was repaired and handed back to me.

During the winter that followed, I managed to play a little hockey and made the mistake of taking some of the team, in my repaired car, to Kroonstad for a game on Sunday. Both the Welkom men's and women's teams were playing that same day: the men in the morning and the women in the afternoon.

I had never been drinking before driving until that day, and it was almost impossible not to be sociable both at lunchtime, after our game, and then following the girls' match in the afternoon and a little more alcohol into the night (though I didn't drink as quickly or as many as I usually would).

A part of the evening's fun was a challenge from a woman on Kroonstad's side who said she could beat every member of our men's team in a boat race (each drinking a pint of lager as quickly as possible).

Normally, it would be equal numbers on each side, but four of our team had already left when the challenge was made. So it was seven individuals drinking one pint each against one woman drinking seven pints one after the other.

To our shame, she won! I still don't know how, as I certainly could not have managed such a feat.

I did not appreciate just how much I might be affected, particularly by taking part in this game just before I left with my three passengers.

Fortunately, I only saw one other car on the fifty-mile journey home in the dark although, soon after setting off, I actually saw four white lines because it was then that I first found out that I suffered from double vision in each eye! (Fortunately, it is only in my later years that I needed glasses for the same condition.)

Seeing four white lines on the road is not very good, so I closed one eye and chose the line on the left in my one working eye, as my guide for most of the journey, remarkably arriving back at our lodgings in one piece.

A bizarre tradition of President Steyn was to throw a party for all white employees who had worked on a particular shaft during the period that ran up to the achievement of one million fatality-free shifts.

I say bizarre because, not only was there a braai, or barbecue, when T-bone steaks were on offer but an almost unlimited supply of cold lager too. This happened after the end of the shift when the miners emerged from underground, and included office staff like surveyors, of which of course I was one, if they wished. Consequently, almost everyone partook of the free booze and then had the pleasure of a drunken drive home afterwards. Strangely, despite the inebriation, I never heard of anyone having an accident and certainly not a fatality.

I don't remember exactly when it happened but fortunately not after the kind of event above but certainly a few days later, as I left work to drive back to my digs, the bright sunshine began to disappear. It was like a dark brown cloud seemingly rushing towards me as I started on my drive.

Then suddenly it was upon me. Not cloud or fog but a dust storm that made it almost impossible to see the road. Of course, I had never seen this phenomenon before and had no idea what to do. But I did decide to slow down almost to a walk, headlights on, because I knew I had to turn left sometime soon. Fortunately, it blew through before I encountered the junction from the mine onto the main road, leaving a thin residue of sand everywhere.

I continued to play hockey during the winter, playing on the left wing, normally for the seconds, but more often this season, I played for the firsts. We really wanted to win the league but had only a few very talented players, but we did have the Free State's goalie on our side and that helped. Anyway, we all agreed to get as fit as possible as this was the best chance of achieving our goal. So, every weekday evening, before the lager and the usual enormous evening meal, we youngsters ran, walked, jogged and ran again as fast as we could for nearly an hour, then did a little practice.

Unfortunately, we didn't come top, but second in the league was quite a good improvement on what we had been used to. Good players on the opposition were often surprised by how quickly they would be surrounded when they were on the ball.

The only thing that did not go well was during another 'friendly' game: men's seconds against our women's team.

I frequently managed to get past my opposing fullback with the ball. Towards the end of the game, she got fed up with this and deliberately hit my right ankle with the bottom of her stick. This really hurt, but I hobbled on.

The pain was worse the next day, so I went to see my doctor, who sent me for an x-ray. This revealed another hairline fracture, for which I was bandaged.

It was such a nuisance as I continued to do my job but had the problem of having to bandage myself up twice a day after showers; once at home and once after coming up from underground was an extra burden I could well do without.

Before the 1968 cricket season started, there was a notice sent around the clubs for anyone who wanted to train to be a certificated umpire.

I took this up and became, if I remember correctly number 97, to be awarded the South African Cricket Umpire's Association qualification.

Subsequently, I umpired a number of first-team league matches and a couple of Country Districts (the equivalent of English County Second XI) games.

One was a friendly two-day match, again at Kroonstad, the Free State Country Districts against Witwatersrand University. One of their team had just been selected for the South African team to tour and play England. That was shortly after called off because of the Basil D'Oliveira affair.

Unfortunately, I can't remember his name but, on the second day, this left-arm spin bowler was bowling from my end when he took a sharp return catch, which dislocated his spinning finger.

He never had an opportunity to play for his country after that.

At this time, I was also President Steyn Cricket Club's honorary secretary and event organiser. I had a busy time, particularly because we worked on Saturday mornings then, and even if I was umpiring or playing the occasional match, one Saturday a month there was a dance or something similar to manage: location, refreshments, a bar and band as well as tickets to organise, and then to look after the event itself.

However, this period also saw an event that changed my life.

During the years, I talked as much as I could with my African staff, but that was always when we could not be seen or heard by a more senior white official because either I would be in trouble, or someone would blame one of my team and threaten them with violence.

I was interested in their beliefs and life at home. They didn't much like talking about home but explained about reincarnation and some other beliefs and rules within their different tribes.

Largely, they seemed to me to be quite similar to those of our English Middle Ages, even if they were now in an industrial era, and had books, newspapers and the radio to listen to.

This was brought home to me on 21 July, after I recorded live Neil Armstrong saying, "This is one short step for man but one giant leap for mankind," when he stepped onto the moon, on top of the Rolling Stones track: 2,000 light years from home.

When, the next morning, I told my team that there was a man actually on the moon, they just laughed and said, "You're making that up baas. You're joking aren't you?" It was hard to convince them otherwise.

Another time I was about to drive into town when I saw one of our waiters, 'Medulla' or an old man, looking distressed and hurrying somewhere, so I stopped and asked if he would like a lift. He explained that he was late getting home for something, so I told him to jump in.

At first, he seemed reticent: looking all around him, before getting in beside me, probably because either, or both of us, might have been shouted at for this misdemeanour.

When we arrived at his home in the African township outside Welkom, he introduced me to his wife who thanked me profusely for my kindness.

I felt very strange when I went back into town. Was it guilt that I had broken some kind of unwritten law about helping a black man, and might have some kind of comeback for it? Or was it that I had done the right thing and now felt good about it, and it was the opposing thoughts that were troubling me?

The confusion continued when I was driving home from the town centre, where I had stopped to buy something, and I felt a kind of physical tension around my body as well a kind of dancing mind in my brain.

Even writing this allows my body and mind to feel and see these mixed emotions all over again. It is very weird sorting out what is right in the circumstances that existed in South Africa at that time.

Was it in part the events of a few months earlier that made me feel the way I did now?

Anyway, I had not been working with my current crew very long and was not to be with them much longer.

This was because some months before, Tom Schimper came into Protea House to see me as I was having my breakfast.

He sat down beside me and asked if I wouldn't mind swapping jobs with him because the day before he had made a mistake—very unusual for him—and needed to put it right at once. He promised to complete my job as well as it was very close by. He would use my boys, and I his.

I was happy to agree as his jobs were usually quite straightforward, and he normally got back on the surface early, so I was looking forward to an easy day. The added bonus was his job was on Four Shaft, so I had an extra half hour before I had to leave for work, and didn't have to hurry down my food either.

I was feeling a form of elation and almost danced out of Protea House to get into my car and off to the mine. It was a bright sunny day, too, and that made the journey all the better.

I was still very cheerful when I got to three shafts as it was the cleanest and the most spacious of the changing rooms, and every stope had fairly high rooves due to the extraordinary thickness of the reef, making it easy to work in them.

This was only the second time I had gone the six thousand feet to the bottom and then gone past the vast cavern that had been created to put in a refrigeration unit to cool the air for the mine workers at the lower levels, as the rock here was quite warm to the touch.

The job was so simple—just one peg to put in—and it took less than two hours to complete the going down in the cage, a further couple of hundred feet down, using an incline shaft, and perhaps a quarter of a mile to the raise to put in the peg and mark up the target for the miner and suddenly, it seemed, I was back on the surface, a little after ten, and back in the welcoming, morning sunlight.

While I was in the shower I heard and felt a small rumble. It was not that unusual, and I thought nothing of it. Then I got dressed and travelled back to the office.

On the way, I saw Tom's gang walking back to their accommodation by Two Shaft and offered them a lift, but they refused because of possible reprisals for taking advantage of a white man's generosity.

Anyway, I parked up near the offices and walked into the surveyor's room. The chief was away, and I can't remember exactly who it was who called me into his office.

I was surprised at the apparent urgency: had someone seen me talking to Tom's boys? Had I done something else wrong? But neither of these was the cause.

"There's been an explosion on 1A Shaft, and there's no one else here, and it needs to be measured up as soon as possible. Have you got your kit with you?" The unremembered face asked.

It was like a shutter came down, cutting off the daylight, and awakening a kind of dread in my mind. Not least because I had never done a job like this before but knew the importance of it, which itself began to weigh me down.

I explained about swapping jobs, and that Tom's boys would be here soon.

He said he would get them brought to the office, and it would be best if I could take Tom's boys with me to One Shaft, where any changing for 1A was done.

As soon as I saw them coming, I left the office and took them to my car. They would have a ride in it after all. Then we hurried over to One Shaft, so I could change into my clothes that were still in the piccaneen's bag. Fortunately, where I had been earlier was warm or just a little bit cool, so my clothes were dry, if a little bit dirty, so they were reasonably comfortable.

Then it was a half-mile ride on a train from One Shaft to 1A.

When we got there, we were immediately lowered to the same level that I should have been on to do my job that morning. By the time I and Tom's boys arrived at the right level, it was about an hour after the explosion had taken place.

I didn't know then where exactly the explosion had taken place, but a shift boss greeted me as I got out of the cage and told me which crosscut to go to.

Then the potential enormity of my task really hit me—it was where my job had been.

Another blow followed as the shift boss stepped aside to let me pass—I was totally shocked by what I thought I saw. I didn't really believe it at first: there was actually a pile of perhaps fifteen or more badly charred bodies, piled on top of each other in three layers, in a corner in front and to my right, just at the start of the haulage entrance from the station.

Later I discovered that a young trainee sampler had been killed in the explosion. I had spoken to him for the first time only the evening before when he told me that he had only been at President Steyn for a month, and today would be his last shift, as he didn't like the work and wanted to go home. He was just nineteen but had no idea what he would do when he got there.

Almost certainly one or more of my trusted and trusting gang were there somewhere: my well-educated, very pleasant and helpful Tangyanikan boss-boy who had a family back home, as well as my, a bit lazy, except when dancing while playing the mouth organ at the same time, piccaneen, and the very quiet but amiable other older member of my team, the names of whom I forget now.

But thoughts of them then were suppressed because of the unwritten norm in this strange world that I worked in, where you had to dismiss any thoughts of this kind; otherwise, I would have been unable to carry out my task.

Tom's team followed me down the haulage. I could hear their shocked voices as we passed the bodies, but they spoke in a language I didn't understand.

Apart from us plodding along in our boots, there was not a sound to be heard. It seemed so strange given that I later learnt that twenty-nine people had been killed and many more injured by the blast.

Presumably, the immediate urgency was to get those showing any sign of life out first, leaving the definitely dead for later.

The silence remained as we continued down the haulage until I saw the first sign of the explosion: a scatter of dark marks on my right side and a scrap of torn faded blue cloth in the gully below. When we got close to the crosscut, I looked more closely at a couple more black marks opposite the entrance and saw that they were actually bits of human skin.

I then had to go back a bit and record any others there had been, marking their locations on the right-hand side wall, presumably where some of the dead or injured persons had been thrown by the force of the explosion. There were also odd dark splatterings of blood, but most of the other evidence here seemed to have been cleaned up if there had been any more.

I was bemused by how little there was to be seen, given that an explosion of this magnitude had only recently occurred—a little more than an hour earlier.

Then we turned left into the crosscut where more evidence could be seen. Again there were no other people that we could see or hear. It seemed totally unreal—a proper deathly silence when we stopped, so I could look around and decide how to carry out the more detailed part of recording the scene.

What was also very strange was the uniformity of the strangely light-grey rock around us. Perhaps it was because of the fireball that the explosion created that had somehow cleaned any dark marks from the walls and roof. Perhaps it was just me or that new lights seemed to have been put up to aid the evacuation of dead and injured.

At least these thoughts helped put my feelings away somewhere deep within me so that they would not interfere with what I was charged to do.

Two of Tom's team reeled out the measuring tape again below two numbered pegs, so that I could begin marking down what could be seen, and at what point along the tape, left or right, how far off line, how high on the wall, and if it was on the roof or footwall so that I could later paint a three-dimensional picture of the scene, for the Mine Inspector to use in his later accident report.

Examples of what I noted were: close to the crosscut entrance there was a boot stuck under the start of the siding's railway line, with a broken off foot and blooded ankle still inside it, together with a few more pieces of skin, somehow stripped from different individuals and stuck to the walls, bits of cloth of different colours, partly charred, mostly lying on the ground or against the walls or in the drain, and, by the rails on my right, Tom's glasses, and nearby, his grey and a shift boss's red hard hats. Then Tom's notebook, open and bloodied, in the waterless ditch next to the railway line but strangely no sign of his pencil.

By now, we were approaching the entrance to the boxhole on our right that was being excavated upwards, and where Tom was supposed to have been working that morning, to amend the measurements he had taken the day before.

Just before the entrance, there was a red-painted electric fan tube which was still limply hanging down on chains with a broken electric cable dangling beneath it and, nearby, bits of the now disconnected light grey metal pipes normally taking fresh air into the nearby boxhole also in something of a jumble and silent now.

This ventilation system was about sixty feet into the crosscut and was almost certainly the source of the explosion when the fan had been switched on to get rid of the methane gas in the boxhole next to it, where Tom was supposed to be going with the shift boss.

My target had been further on in the stope itself, but it would have been normal for me to have stopped for a chat with the shift boss before entering the stope I was supposed to have been working in that day.

Although the electric motor was supposed to be shielded from the possibility of a spark, a spark from it, or the nearby switch, must have been how the explosion was triggered when it was switched on, judging by the way that various bits and pieces appeared to have been thrown away from either side of it. But, of course, it was also possible that the spark could have occurred from the cable attached to it that had not been properly attached.

It was surprising, given the power of the blast, how these remains seemed almost intact, while I noted the absence of the strong airtight doors that should have been in front of me.

However, the explosion occurred, it was certainly very powerful because the pair of ventilation doors, just twenty feet or so beyond the fan motor, had been completely destroyed. The only sign that the two doors had once been there were some broken, light grey breeze blocks still cemented to the rock, creating a couple of shattered picture frames.

The two doors themselves had been made of wooden planks, about two inches thick, and with sturdy flat iron bars holding them together, as well as strong hinges attached to the wood frame and light grey breezeblocks that were cemented together and to the rock around them. This formed, as near as possible, an airtight chamber, where only one door could be open at one time—as I had discovered while training.

Apart from a few shattered breeze blocks further towards the stope entrance, there were a couple of yellow and black bits of doors but no sign of their reinforcing metal bars. Unless most of the doors and blocks had been vaporised, the bulk of the debris must have had to be removed, possibly because of the number of people who had been killed or injured beyond the doors. Indeed, I discovered damage as far as forty feet inside the stope itself, where I would have been working, if I had got there at all because Tom and I would have arrived together had he not had the job on three shafts to do, then both of us would have been near the site of the fan being switched on, to allow Tom to 'safely' go into the boxhole, while I continued into the stope to do my job.

Given what I had already written down, more than twenty deaths must have occurred near or at the top of the raise below our level, but there was nothing obvious to see where the bodies had been or how they might have died, for me to be able to record.

Given the evidence from around where the doors had stood, debris from the blast may well have been the likely cause of their demise.

Bizarrely, a red miner's box was sitting, unmoved, just beyond where the second door had been.

I often wonder how the obviously substantial quantity of methane had built up, and how neither a shift boss nor the white miner had checked for it earlier than when the explosion occurred, as would normally have been the procedure.

Of course, methane can occur in gold mines but, as far as I was aware, it didn't happen very often. When it did it was usually associated with a fault in the rock.

Certainly, I saw evidence of a significant fault nearby, indeed the boxhole may have been a future travelling way to get at the reef, if it had been thrown upward back somewhere in time, or it was simply going up to connect to a recently mined raised going up to the next level to do its normal job. Either way, it was not part of my job to make a geological report, as the Geology Office would already have the necessary data that could easily be added for the mine investigator to look at.

I never asked about the cause, nor was the Inspector's later report clear about the possible cause of the build-up. This was normal for reports because they almost never placed any blame on anyone and certainly neither the managers nor the mine owners.

Even after a black worker jumped onto an ordinary truck and held a metal bar up to the overhead electric cable that normally powered an electric engine with the idea that that was all that was necessary to drive the truck forward, was any report issued, I heard, despite the black man's unnecessary death.

There were not even any safety recommendations made after that event that I knew about. Perhaps it was this sort of behaviour or lack of understanding of the power of electricity and similar things or maybe tribal beliefs that made many white people think of those who were black or coloured as less than them and consequently behave in a sometimes almost inhuman way themselves by the way they treated these people?

It was certainly hard for those with a European education to know what was or was not possible in this unfamiliar world.

When I at last got back to the office, I learnt that Tom had 95% burns. He died two days after arriving at the hospital. He was one of the twenty nine fatalities that also included my lovely gang.

I really missed my Tanganyikan boss-boy, who was always so polite, interesting and kind, so it was easy to treat much as an equal as I dared for the time he was with me. My piccanine, while he could be lazy and annoying, was not only funny at times but a proficient musician; playing a mouth organ while dancing at the same time to entertain some of his friends after work. The other member was always so quiet that you wouldn't know he was there, except that he always did his job quietly and efficiently, even seeming to anticipate our needs before I or my boss-boy asked for him to do them.

These thoughts kept coming to me in the following days as, to me, we seemed a bit like a family, and to lose these members was a tremendous shock, though hide that I must, I told myself.

I also had no way of contacting the families of my team to tell them just what lovely people they were, particularly my boss-boy, as he had a lot of promise and ability, but unfortunately, he was not able to make use of his skills in his own country.

These thoughts added to my feelings of guilt at their demise.

I just can't remember exactly what else I thought during the following days. My mind must have been so affected by what I had seen and recorded, as well as the thought that it was likely I would have been killed that day if Tom had not asked me to change jobs and had not gone to tackle his correction in the raise first before the work assigned to me that morning, and which also meant that I was assigned to measure up the site of the catastrophe.

What made matters even worse over the following weeks, was that Tom's wife had been given a kind of non-job to do, so that she had some money coming in, and something to do after losing her husband. (I did not ask, but it seemed there was no kind of insurance payment made to the wife of an employee after a fatality.) But it also meant that I frequently saw her around the offices, which always reminded me of the image of Tom at breakfast and later his glasses and blooded notebook in the crosscut that still haunted me, as well as the change of places and the question: 'Why not me?'

I withdrew into a kind of shell but couldn't work out quite why. It seemed that all my energy and enthusiasm for anything in my life had gone. Having the three roles of surveying, my job within President Steyn Cricket Club to organise social events and cricket umpiring was a combination that finally drove me to hand in my notice. Even the idea of playing hockey at the start of the new season was no joy to me.

I just felt too guilty, too often.

I also began to worry that, had it been me going to the crosscut on my own, the explosion would probably not have happened at all, as the shift boss would not have needed to switch on the fan to the raise, so would not have been there either.

But then the work tunnelling the raise would have been stopped until Tom or someone else went to make the necessary corrections.

At this thought, I became more befuddled as the 'what ifs' would not go away, and the feeling of guilt got harder to bare.

So I made up my mind to leave, without thinking about what I might do for a living. I gave a month's notice and soon one day I was working in the mine and the next travelling to Johannesburg with no idea what to do there. Of course, I had to give some notice, but when I explained the situation I was in, it only took a week, not the month I had expected.

Even fifty years later, the scenes and my feelings come back to me, on occasion.

At least, after I had the conversation, I could think about the future.

What made my decision easier was that I had holiday pay to take, as well as my salary so, with the savings I had put by to travel back to the UK, I thought I would have enough to get by in Johannesburg while I searched for work.

The whole of my time in Welkom was, in some respects, confusing.

It is only now that I wonder how Tom's little gang felt after they help me measure up the disaster underground.

In England, I had seen little racism although my mum, who was born in South Africa, had strong views about black people. But I tried to put them to one side until I found out for myself what people of colour were like.

The only place I had seen people who were not white was in London, and then only in passing. So all I could go by was what I had seen on television; from films or documentaries, neither of which had prepared me for my introduction to the black African workers I had seen at the station upon arrival in Welkom.

One colour film my brother took me to see when I was seven or eight, and still living in Headcorn, was shown in the village hall. In it were scenes of the Mau Mau in Kenya capturing a farmer and beheading him. It must have had some sort of effect on me to be able to recall this nearly seventy years later, but I can't remember it affecting me while in South Africa.

Perhaps my first real sight of mine workers was in the early morning of my arrival in Welkom. It jogged my memory a little bit when I thought I had been taken back decades in time, seeing the reception that our train got from the waiting prospective customers. However, what they were doing looked like pleasure, not harm.

In itself, this was not real—it did not convey what they were like as people like me. It was a harp back to former days and did not show the character and humanity I found when working with them. Although the occasional incident showed that some of their histories still had a part to play in their lives, particularly for those who knew little or nothing of what there was outside the village and only the tribal systems that still pertained.

Then, in Protea House, finding the black Africans who worked there exceedingly polite, understanding and pleasant but, of course, distant because of their position.

Nevertheless, occasionally someone new to Protea House would appear in the dining room, and treat these people in a totally unnecessary way: shouting at them if the food was not just how they wanted it, as if the waiter should have known his exact wishes. It was extremely annoying for me to hear such tetchiness and even swearing at them, when it was never the waiter's fault, if any fault there actually was.

I didn't have the guts, but I felt like going over to him and, at the very least, shouting at him for his unjustified behaviour. I was sure he would not speak to a white worker in the same way.

However, one day, a few days after the explosion, for a second time I offered 'Madulla' (or old man) a lift to his home in the township because he looked a bit unwell, and I knew his home was some distance walk away. He tried to decline, but I insisted that he got in the car which, finally, he did. (For me to do this was generally frowned upon by most white South Africans.)

Then I almost invited myself into his home for a proper look when we got there because I wanted to see what it was like. He was a bit reluctant but eventually agreed. Apart from it being small for a full-sized family, it looked beautifully comfortable and a real credit to him and his wife despite the low pay they had to live on.

I let him know what I thought of the house and medulla and received a wonderful smile from both him and his wife in return.

Going back to my first impressions; when going underground by myself for the first time, being confronted by a scene that I could not believe, and having great difficulty deciding what to say to the white miner in front of me, I was so very shocked.

It was only when I got my own group of workers who, at first, I wasn't sure I could fully trust that I started to understand where they were coming from.

Few had had the opportunity of going to the kind of school where I had learnt a little about the world about me but mostly academic subjects. I also had the Home Service and television to help me understand something of the wider world. Little of this had been available to the tribal areas in southern Africa until fairly recently, and even then the stations were run by white people with their ideas and culture.

It took some time for both of us to trust each other, and particularly my team trusting me not to be violent, and even think of their welfare underground.

It was only when they heard me being shouted at for trying to talk to them that they began to open up a bit, and I began to find out how similar in many ways our cultures and beliefs were.

Of course, the big difference was that many of these workers had come from remote, still tribal villages, in an attempt to get some money for their families.

Some of the sanctions their elders, who ruled the little regions, had were brutal. I was very surprised by some of them but I find it difficult to remember any more than this general feeling I had.

Indeed some actions were inter-tribal, as I mentioned earlier.

There was also the problem of language. My knowledge of the made-up language of Fanakalo was scant, and mainly applied to the work environment and, apart from schoolboy French, that was it. However, for some illogical reason, I expected that they had a grasp of English. If anything, they knew some Afrikaans, which I did not.

So communication was sometimes difficult but, with a little patience and listening to their ideas at times when I could, had its reward. Thankfully, I always had an English-speaking boss-boy who could sometimes translate what others in the team had to say, depending on his own command of the language but only one of the three who were appointed to me had full understanding.

No wonder it was hard going to find things out by talking. The way I did get to know their character was how they largely behaved among themselves, and with me underground.

I think they started to trust me when I always led the way into unknown or potentially dangerous situations. I never told one of them to go first to see if they got killed or injured. I tried to treat them as equals despite the criticism I received from some quarters.

So my overall impression was that there was little to choose between us in many important respects, and I found it hard to ever think of them as inferior, apart from their lack of general knowledge or things happening elsewhere in the world.

This understanding helped me later on in life, when back in England, during four years of management in one of my appointments, of the full-time staff I had, I was the only one originally from the UK. I always listened to the problems any member of staff had and then asked to see what the difficulty was for myself so that I could either solve the matter myself or explain to another what was needed, like a different type of machine. When I had another management job, I also did things like employing only those whose application and CV would normally have been filed in the waste bin: they had the skills I needed, but I only found that out by interviewing them—and they turned out to be excellent and reliable staff. I was also as flexible as I could be if someone needed time off, or to change hours; where possible I asked such changes to be agreed with another colleague in return for helping that person out if necessary. However, when one member of staff came in with a very concerned look on his face and told me his wife had given birth to triplets when only one baby had been expected, I told him to have the week off still on full pay. In those days, there was no such requirement for employers.

This way I knew that my staff would help out at any time if they could and that I would get the best out of them.

This goes back to what I thought about the treatment I saw given to a black mine worker in my early days underground.

Later, when I became a lecturer in management, one forty-three-year-old man, who had been a butcher's boy for twenty-three years, with no academic qualifications, having left school at fifteen, and poor reading and writing skills, then moved to work on a production line. His new employer gave their staff an opportunity to learn leadership and management skills on a programme that I had designed and taught. He managed to gain a degree equivalent to management qualification.

Perhaps this was because he was able to talk to me at any time about the plans he had, including a couple of midnights on a Sunday! Or he would ask me to visit the factory so that he could show me and explain what he was proposing. That meant that he had a better idea of how to construct his plan in writing as part of his evidence, particularly because I asked him questions that made him realise that his explanation had to be clear to anyone else reading his thesis, who did not know what his workplace was like, in order that my assessment could be verified by the awarding body.

Anyway, as a result, four years after starting as a production line worker, he was appointed production manager for an international paint manufacturing company, with a big jump in income.

The thing I could never come to terms with when I worked in the mine, was the complete absence of mental support, or even interest in my well-being after any of the traumatic events I had been through. I simply had to manage my feelings myself and get on with it. Otherwise, I only remember receiving a couple of compliments about my work during the whole time I was a surveyor.

This applied both at work and within Protea House. However, when I was made aware of anyone else I knew who was having a problem, I would always try to help them by listening—it seemed to do me good as well.

This was something else that helped me when I was later a manager.

Now, however, it was time for me to have a new adventure in Johannesburg.

I managed to pack everything I owned into my car, somehow including my trunk containing my, by now, quite substantial record collection, plus my Revox tape deck. The rest of my limited clothing got into my case and a couple of bags.

When I rang my cousin to ask if I could stay for a bit, I had been offered a short stay with her and her family again until I found a place to live.

This was my first endeavour to find accommodation, as I didn't really want to take advantage of her and her husband's goodwill. However, the fact that I could play chess with him seemed to make me a little less of a nuisance.

Rosemary and her husband were very kind, but I knew that I couldn't stay for very long, and hunted in the papers for somewhere to live within reasonable distance of town.

Eventually, I found a very nice but quite pricy place compared with Protea House, and I knew that the remains of my funds would not last long without work.

At that time, there seemed to be few jobs in the papers, and because it promised the possibility of a quite good income, I was drawn to an advertisement for people to sell the Encyclopaedia Britannica.

The interview was more like a sales pitch than what I had expected, and it was only after taking on the job that promised much that I realised that it was more or less a con. Yes, you could earn quite a lot if you sold well but, even with a well-tried pitch to help you, it was no easy task.

I was put into a team with three others and our leader decided where to go to find our marks. Usually, this was in the poorer areas around Johannesburg where you looked for people who wanted some way of improving the chances for their children.

One family that I remember particularly had three or four children. The parents were very keen and interested in what I was offering them, and quite happily signed up for what I reckoned was the maximum that they could afford for any one thing in a year.

There was a cosy but obviously cheap house with well-worn furniture, and I felt very guilty after they had agreed to buy.

They were Afrikaaners, people who usually despised the English, but these people spoke very good English and seemed down on their luck as well as very polite. They and their home reminded me more of Madulla's home than those of other whites' I visited.

One of our trips took us out for a weekend to somewhere near Lydenburg, where we hoped that country people would be more willing to part with their cash than most other places we went to. We were wrong, and after two days, only two sets had been sold.

To make matters worse, something went wrong with the people carrier that was also our home. Or it may have been simple tiredness by our driver and leader, as we started to head back towards Jo'burg in the growing dark. Whatever the real reason, we found a police station and asked if there was any accommodation nearby.

There was none, but the only officer around kindly offered us a night in the cells.

How could we refuse? It had to be better than trying to sleep in the carrier again.

We were ushered into a room, a cell is a better word for it, about thirty feet square, with a tiny window more than twenty feet up on one wall, and a single light bulb in the middle of the ceiling. All the walls and the ceiling were painted black, and the only comfort was straw strewn around the floor for us to sleep on.

I can't remember if there were any other facilities, but there must have been at least a latrine and a cold water tap because, in the morning soon after being woken by last night's friendly policeman, there was a short delay for a use of the facilities, and for our driver to tinker with something in the engine, then we were off for a two- or three-hour drive back to the city.

Another incident occurred when we were taken to another location somewhere in the outback.

Our driver dropped me off first at a crossroad about half a mile from a little hamlet, if you could reasonably call the scattered group of houses and farms that. Having disembarked, he told me to meet the people carrier back at the crossroads at about nine o'clock that evening.

After a fruitless trudge along a number of dirt tracks, and many refusals, it was now getting dark as I approached the pick-up point, but the sky was clear with a nearly full moon to light the ground, and I stood and waited on one corner by a ditch.

The night being absolutely still, just a slight noise in the ditch made me look down. There I saw a dark, shadowy snake moving slowly towards me.

This was not a moment when I could take my time to work out whether it was dangerous or not, so I quickly crossed to the opposite corner to wait once more.

Only a couple of minutes later I felt something against my open-toed sandals, and a quick glance down indicated the unmistakeable black shape of a scorpion. Once more, after a quick kick, I was off to the next corner.

By now, I wasn't too sure from which direction my lift would be coming, as I looked this way and that for any sign of rescue. However, the only movement I detected was once more when I looked down on the ground—there was a large, hairy spider just sitting there, possibly trying to work out whether my feet were worth further investigation or not.

Whatever it was thinking, I was remembering an earlier encounter with a much smaller version that had bitten me, so off to the last corner where, fortunately, I only had minutes to wait before the lights and shape of my rescue came into view and picked me up.

No one would believe me when I told the other occupants what had happened while I waited.

During this period of encyclopaedia selling, I met one of my colleagues and got to know Johannes Schule quite well. One day he told me that he was going to rent a small flat and asked if I would like to share it with him.

As it happened the manager of the property where I had a room for rent had called me one morning a few days earlier. I had failed to pay for the next month's rent on time, and the only thing I could do was try to get an overdraft.

My lack of success both in selling or finding a job, meant that my funds were running low, and I was also called into my bank. There I was met by the manager who spoke to me in Afrikaans, even though he knew I was English and he could speak the language quite well. He was also quite threatening, so I told him I would take my account elsewhere, even though

I knew that my next rent would not be covered by what was left in the bank.

It also left me to find another job urgently, and fortunately, one came up that I thought I could do: doing market research for Market Research Africa. I was not sure whether it was salaried or piece work, but there was always some research to do, and I was able to persuade a different bank's manager that it was alright for him to take on a customer, now with an overdraft already in tow.

This allowed me both to cover whatever rent I owed and take up the offer of sharing the flat with Johannes when, a couple of days later, I bumped into him and he asked me to come round to the flat in a block called Mount Ararat, near Hillbrow. This would be good as it was within walking distance of where we both worked and was much cheaper than where I was living.

Johannes was a Swiss, so spoke French, German and English fluently as well as Swiss, and sometimes switched to a different language than English, when he wanted a particular phrase that was not easily translated to English or he did not know the equivalent. It was both quite amusing and to some extent our conversations were often more interesting because of this.

I found the market research interview interesting and quite enjoyable, except when I was asked to compare the taste of two different brands of sweetcorn. Stupidly, I consumed all the contents of both cans. After doing that, it was impossible to tell them apart. I have avoided eating sweet corn, if possible, ever since.

One of my more interesting assignments involved finding out reactions from people to a choice of design for a new type of tissue box.

Unlike previous packs of tissues that were rectangular and fairly flat, these were a square box shape. The two designs available were dice, with the colour of the tissues as the dots, or ordinary white in a leafy floral kind of patterned box.

By far, the best response was for the dice that people said could be used in an office or anywhere around the house, and not at all gender-specific.

Anyway, work aside, I was very grateful for sharing with Johannes as he was meticulous with money, keeping a record of everything we spent for living in the flat down to the penny. Now not only was my share of the rent much less than I was paying before, but my cost of feeding myself was considerably lower too.

This was essential because my then income just about covered my costs.

More than that, Johannes liked to cook all the evening meals, which were both tasty and economical. We even had enough to buy a case of lager and a bottle of brandy a week.

One of my colleagues from the research company asked for a lift home one day, so I took him to his house out in the country that was a bit like a disused farmhouse.

A couple of days later he invited me back there.

When I arrived I saw a large dog near the front door and thought little of it until I knocked on the door. The dog, still with a chain around its neck rushed forward, breaking the chain from where it was tied, and leapt at me, sinking its teeth mainly into my jacket sleeve.

It was still hanging grimly onto my elbow and shaking it a bit when, at last, my friend's mother came to the door. With hardly a glance at the dog, she asked, "What do you want?"

I told her that her son [I've forgotten his name, but not the situation] had asked me to call round that afternoon.

Still ignoring the dog hanging from my jacketed arm, she replied a little crossly, "He's gone out." At which she turned her back on me, and left me with the dog.

Fortunately, as I turned right to try and leave, the dog let go of my elbow as if that's okay then and went nonchalantly back to his kennel!

When I looked later, I found only bruising where the dog's teeth had been. I never saw the lad again as good fortune changed my life once more.

A couple of weeks earlier, I had gone to the library to see if I could find a job that would interest me.

While browsing I happened to notice a fairly thick, green-backed book that seemed like a small encyclopaedia of jobs. It was right on the top shelf, and as I reached up and tried to grasp it, it slipped from my hand and fell open on the floor.

When I picked it up, still open as it had fallen, the first job title I saw was that of 'copywriter'.

I was intrigued and read on. The more I read, the more it excited me, particularly as it stated that some knowledge of market research would be useful, and of course, I had a little and had also done some face-to-face selling. So I thought that I had a bit of useful experience behind me. I also thought that several advertisements that I had read recently in newspapers were not particularly good.

Then I looked around the library and borrowed two or three books talking about the skills of writing advertisements.

In the next few days, I read them copiously and also scanned the papers for adverts that I thought could be improved, several of which I cut out.

Having looked carefully at my amendments and my reasons for them, I bought a folder and put them in along with their corresponding ads. Then I looked in a telephone directory to find the names and addresses of advertising companies in Jo'burg, wrote them down and set off one sunny Monday to try to sell myself by knocking on doors.

After three setbacks because of no vacancies, but two telling me to keep in touch, I went to E Lindsay-Smithers on Commissioner Street.

Somewhat to my surprise, after a phone call to the creative director's office by the receptionist, I was immediately invited up to see him. Previously, I had only spoken to lesser beings in the other agencies.

Even more surprising was an offer to start work as soon as I could, having been cross-questioned about my ideas for improvement of the advertisements that I had shown him. I couldn't have done better because this was the largest practitioner in advertising in South Africa.

I almost floated out of his office and along the road to the market research company I worked for to hand in my notice, saying goodbye to the Chinese receptionist, who continued to be an occasional friend.

On Monday, I arrived at the ad agency, went to the lifts and up to their floor, where the receptionist smiled at me and called the number for the creative director.

He came along, smiling as well, and gave me a warm greeting, then took me along the corridor and down the one to the right where, he explained, all the copywriters were. To the left were the visualisers and a photographic studio.

My office was the last on the right down the corridor, and shared with two others, each of us screened from the other, my place being just inside the door and on the left.

I had a very comfortable soft secretary's seat, a dark wooden desk, with a telephone and an old sit-up-and-beg black typewriter, in which to catch my fingers between the keys, and a pile of blank white paper in a wire basket for me to use.

I was the first to arrive in the room that morning, but soon, my neighbours arrived, along with a tea trolley and someone else with a small pile of magazines, which he distributed among us.

After the greetings, the two others; a male a few years older than me, whose little box was beside mine and a senior female, with a bigger space than ours and a separate door. Their names I forget (I've always been bad at remembering people's names) but both were pleasant enough when we did speak. Then they went to their own desks to read through the magazines and had their cuppas.

This was a normal start to the day while we waited for the day's assignments. Generally, there was little action before ten o'clock unless there was something urgent to finish or I had a meeting to go to.

My first day was more concerned with getting signed in and meeting some of the visualisers, with whom I would be working, to get some idea of the routine.

Normally, a copywriter and visualiser would be shown the brief at about the same time and would get together quickly to exchange immediate views and get some idea of the likely layout, given the size and type of publication they would be going in, as well as how much space I might have for my copy.

My immediate neighbour also showed me what he was working on, and what the procedures were regarding the finished copy being checked.

After the lunch break, someone came to the door and handed me a folder with my first job, quickly followed by the person who was to do the artwork and layout.

When I looked at it, it was particularly uninspiring, being an advertisement for GKN Scaffolding, where we had to use the picture that the company had supplied. The brief also stated where the advertisement would appear: a building trade magazine. Perhaps this was the least interesting assignment I ever had. They had even included an example of the copy they wanted!

What, I wondered, was I to do with that?

As I was reading the brief, the representative dealing with the account popped his head around the corner, introduced himself and explained that the company didn't really want any changes, "Except to make it a bit more interesting to that written in their catalogue."

How on earth could I do that? I wondered but set about making the language a bit more warm and friendly; more like a letter to a friend that I thought would make it stand out from the competition, judging by those from their competitors that I read in a previous copy of the magazine.

I tried a few versions before settling on one that I thought was best, then waited for my neighbour to take another tea break to ask his opinion.

I was pleased that, apart from a couple of minor word changes, he thought it would do the job.

Then I sat back and read more of the magazines that I had been given in the morning until it was time to go home.

The next day, the visualiser brought around a sample of the advertisement that he had finished, with the space for my copy as well as my heading put in.

Shortly afterwards, the rep dropped by to see what we, and particularly I, had done. He looked pleased and thought it would do the job, then took my copy away with him to show to GKN.

I remember being very pleased that my first task had been approved and relaxed with a copy of Billboard to see what the top ten singles were in the USA.

Most days I was supplied with one or more briefs to deal with. Often they were articles companies wanted for magazine placements.

A larger version of this was a large folder for a new five-star hotel in the centre of Johannesburg that already had a number of boutique-like shops on its mezzanine floor that it wanted to highlight.

Although I had heard the news of the building being built, I knew nothing about it. So I asked if I could just pop around to have a look and to try and pick up something similar from a rival hotel to get an idea of what such a brochure might contain.

The creative director seemed pleased to see the enthusiasm I was putting into my work, particularly as my assigned visualiser had not had such a task to do before either.

Together, the visualiser and I sat down to discuss the sample I had obtained, as well as hear my account of the place, in order that we could plan something different but would show something of the class and luxury available.

He also planned what kind of photographs he should use and the type and together about the rough size of the copy I would need to write once the photos were printed.

The aim was to make this hotel at least as good, if not much better than the Savoy in London.

Happily, the eventual product was enthusiastically received by the owners.

However, there was one similar assignment that I will never forget, apart from the company concerned as, when it was published the Managing Director's name had been misspelt!

The name I had copied accurately from the brief, and it had been checked by seven other people before going to print, including our rep and his contact at the company. The error caused a loss of twenty-five thousand Rand (about £12,000 then) to Lindsay-Smithers! But I never got the blame.

E Lindsay-Smithers was probably the largest agency in Africa, with another office in Cape Town, as well as others in other countries in Africa and close arrangements with another agency in London.

Early on I had an assignment to write wording for a new slimming tablet. It was quite a small one, not the tablet itself, and due to be put in a single column in a newspaper's Sunday supplement.

I can't remember the brand name but do remember watching how the obviously experienced, older visualiser dealt with it.

I sat by him at his board as he took two images of the woman who had 'lost this weight'. They were identical until he picked up a pair of scissors and removed pounds from her tummy by some judicious cutting. Then he assembled the pair of original and clipped pictures and fitted my copy and the heading around them.

Apparently, the advertisement was quite effective, and I got a few more of this type of advertisement to do over the year.

Nowadays, such practice is banned, but then it was quite normal but obviously misleading. Nevertheless, I was pleased to be able to point it out to my flatmate, Johannes, and his two German friends, when they visited us for a drink that Sunday. Though I didn't mention how the improvement had happened.

This experience, together with other similar products I was asked to do the copy for during my time in the agency, has led to a healthy doubt about claims made by cosmetic and other company advertising mostly aimed at women.

Often they say things like 90% of women, who tried whatever, agree that they felt that the product made their faces, for example, much smoother. That may be the case, but it is obvious that no objective testing has been done to support such a claim. Often the sample used is quite small if it is even given. There is also the possibility that the sample has been selected, and those answering were given some financial or other benefit for their positive responses.

This is simply because women, my wife included, are often gullible when it comes to the possibility of looking younger or more attractive.

The arrangement with Johannes was great too. My income was more than I had to work as an underground surveyor, and as Johannes was meticulous with money, recording every bit of household expenditure to the penny, so I was gradually accumulating funds in my bank account at last.

Although I offered to make the evening meal sometimes, Johannes liked to do it himself, as well as buy all the food and alcohol for the week.

I may say that his food was always very tasty and filling. Of course, I did most of the washing up! Fortunately, we got on very well together, particularly because I had a large collection of singles and LPs, and also a Revox tape recorder and a number of long playing tapes of recordings I had taken from my records. As there was no TV then, my music provided something pleasant in the background.

It was a bit like being back in Protea House but then I was asked to play them quite loudly for the swimmers and sunbathing people outside on the grass to listen to.

They also became background music when different visitors came around for a drink or more in the flat.

Going back to my work as a copywriter, there was one piece of writing that I was asked to do about an industrial company, but I can't remember who. However, what I do remember was being invited to visit their factory, or one of them, so that I would have a feeling of the company when I wrote its background for a publicity leaflet.

When I was taken around, I was very surprised to see a section where fairly sophisticated, manual cutting, drilling, bending, grinding or otherwise shaping of metal was done on machines that obviously required considerable skill to operate.

The surprise was not in the complexity and skill, but in the fact that the operations were carried out in the same large room, with a long, white curtain dividing the white from black engineers.

It was explained to me that there were not enough white people qualified for the work, or interested in doing it, so they had trained black workers to the same skill level in order to keep up with demand. They also paid them the same rates!

In the 1970 Apartheid South Africa, that information amazed me.

However, I was asked not to make any mention of any of this, while stating the level of skill their factory workers had, as I could see by the quality of work being produced.

Going back to life at Lindsay-Smithers, every Friday afternoon the creative staff stopped work early and congregated in the manager's office in the corner of the building next to the corridor to the visualisers' office.

Here, there was a drink laid out for us. I'm not absolutely certain, but I seem to remember some people organising a whip round for more, and on one occasion at least, there were also meat pies on the menu.

On that day, things got a bit out of hand, and instead of all the pies being eaten, many ended up splattering the walls, having missed their target opposite. It was not something that I thought was right, and fortunately, I was not one of the targets, so had no need to retaliate.

Like me, none of the women took part, but the MD told us all that he did not want the same thing to happen again because he had had a number of complaints from the cleaners on the following Monday morning.

It did not register with me until after many such evenings that none of the Afrikaans staff were involved. Indeed, even though they might translate my and my colleagues' writing, they never appeared on our floor at all. The native black African translators also had a floor to themselves—multiple Apartheid here, then.

A few of the younger creative male staff often went up onto the flat roof of the building at lunchtimes to have a little game of cricket, wickets drawn in chalk on the side of the small structure allowing egress from the stairs to this site, and the balls were made up of closely squashed and rounded waste paper that was held in place by sellotape. The bat was either a child's or a roughly shaped piece of wood.

Occasionally the 'ball' was hit over the edge, either to land in the quadrangle surrounded by the offices below or onto Commissioner Street. I often wondered what drivers and pedestrians made of this strange object, like a very odd kind of snowball, descending upon them as they went about their business.

I also wondered about the effect one other incident had.

On or about 5 November 1969, one of our numbers arrived, not with a ball or bat but a large, white, cardboard dart about ten feet long. Stuck underneath it were four large, red-coloured bangers, the size of sticks of gelignite, which had fairly long black fuses, that looked more like curved wire, hanging down from them.

The fuses were lit and the dart set off along Commissioner Street towards the nearby police station. Right on cue, and still at a fair height above the cars, the bangers exploded, right in front of the station.

Unbeknown to those of us on the roof, the Minister of the Interior was meeting our MD, to work out an advertising programme about road safety and watching out for thieves, among other things.

Surprisingly there was no comeback for this little bit of misbehaviour, but we did get told off for dropping the odd banger into the quadrangle, when its explosion would shock all the typists near the windows of offices lower down, causing them to jump and miss-type whatever it was they were typing.

One evening sometime in November, Johannes brought a couple of his German friends round to the flat for a drink. They were polite but mostly spoke in German, so following any of their conversations was nigh impossible, but they tried to include me whenever they could.

As their visits became more frequent they were polite enough to speak English much more, so I could join in the conversations.

Later, Johannes asked me if I would make an English Christmas dinner for him and the two friends. This was to be my first attempt at cooking for anyone else, but I did my best but had to rely on a bought Christmas pudding for the sweet.

Something unexpected and unusual happened on New Year's Day 1970 when I found myself at a large cricket stadium in Johannesburg that I think was the Wanderers but might not be, as photos I have seen from around that date don't quite match my memory.

However, whatever the ground, there was a small tournament for three-man teams, from local clubs, playing in a one-day knock-out competition, which had just started when I arrived. The local club provided fielders so that there were eleven in the field.

This was something I had read about in one of the papers I saw before we broke up from work for the Christmas break.

I'm not sure how it was that I umpired in a couple of matches, I think it was because someone came around, just after the tournament started, to where I and a few other people were sitting, and asked if there was someone who could umpire because one had not arrived, so I, someone SACUA qualified but with only a few months experience, volunteered.

In the first game I was employed, I was umpiring at square leg—at the batsman's end. As usual, I was watching the bowler at the opposite end of me and looked at his arm action very carefully as he delivered the ball. The first ball he bowled seemed slightly wrong, and so was his second, so I changed sides of the wicket to look more carefully from my new position at the point on the offside.

His next ball was normal, and the first to be struck for runs, his next though, I no-balled for throwing. (The one and only time I no-balled anyone for throwing, and something that very, very rarely occurs in cricket matches anywhere around the world—just forty times in international cricket since 1898, so I believe.)

One of the fielders nearby came up to me and almost whispered, "Do you know who that is?"

"No," I honestly answered.

"That's Don Wilson."

I was none the wiser and simply shrugged my shoulders and gave the fielder a weak smile as if I knew the name but had no idea that this was someone famous in the cricketing world, as I did not get newspapers, except if I wanted to show Johannes my work. Otherwise, I rarely read anything about cricket except that being played in South Africa.

The fielder moved back to his fielding position, while I was wondering who he meant.

Thereafter, Don Wilson's bowling action was fine, but more runs were knocked off him per over than in his first, to his obvious annoyance.

Anyway, after the tournament was over, I was having a drink on my own in the bar, when Don Wilson came up to me and tapped me on the shoulder. I turned and still remember the first words he spoke, "You were a very brave young man. (I was just twenty-two then.) I wondered why you moved sides. You are the only person, other than the MCC, to have noticed my bowling action, you know."

Then he walked away as I thanked him for speaking to me. The impression I had was that my action in no-balling him had been quite correct, as there was no hint from him that I might have been wrong.

Only then did I realise from his accent that this was from England. A little later on I asked one of the players in the competition who Don Wilson was. He told me that the man I had no-balled played for Yorkshire and England!

This was a little interlude in our way of life, as most weekends and some evenings, various friends and acquaintances of Johannes visited us for a drink and chat.

Sometimes the conversations were very interesting with people using their own tongue, English or even a range of suitable phrases from English, German and French languages. For me, German was the hardest to follow, but somehow everyone managed to convey what they wanted fairly clearly.

Often sentences became a mixture of languages, as people would sometimes use an odd phrase that they had picked up from hearing others, as they deemed them more appropriate for the image they wanted to create. A couple of months after the November meeting between our management and the

Minister, I was asked by the senior visual artist if I would like to be his model for a photo shoot. I happily agreed as I had nothing urgent to finish.

He took me, his photographic gear and a soft bag, downstairs to his car in the basement car park. Then we drove out to an isolated cottage somewhere on the fringes of Jo'burg.

There he rigged me out with a slightly crumpled, light brown trilby style hat and matching but old oversized raincoat.

Then I was asked to crouch as if trying to find a way in through a bungalow window without being seen. He took a number of shots with me in slightly different positions, and then we went back to the office.

About a month later my picture was on a 'Watch out there's a thief about' poster displayed in every police station in South Africa, among other places, including newspapers.

Fortunately, nobody recognised the 'criminal' and I was never arrested. Perhaps that was in part because my normal form of dress was so different to that on the poster, as I used to wear flared trousers, and often something like a shiny purple shirt, with a complimentary coloured, narrow scarf round my neck.

This dress was to fit in with the idea for our customers that everyone was indeed creative. It worked for me, as I got a number of jobs aligned with the wants of teenagers and young twenties. My language was more akin to that of the pop record-buying public, or so our clients seemed to think.

Apart from work, life with Johannes was always interesting as, apart from anything else, every female he bumped into seemed to fancy him—he certainly had no lack of partners to choose from who would spend the night with him.

This was somewhat galling for me. There was almost no interaction with other female staff at work, other than those in the creative arena, and they were all much older than me, if I met or worked with any apart from the Friday drinks party.

It was only by chance that I might meet anyone I was interested in, or I seemed to interest them. However, our co-existence usually worked very well on almost all fronts until, for some reason or another, one or another lost interest, but it was much better than living in Welkom. At least, from time to time I had female company.

Johannes was meticulous with money in a way that was unexpected, for he had a small notebook in which he kept his and our joint expenditure, and would record every transaction down to the penny.

We had an agreed weekly budget for the flat; food any materials or other articles that we both deemed necessary. I can't remember a single disagreement in this regard.

Alcohol for the week was always first on the list and a case of lager plus a bottle of brandy was usually enough to suffice, though sometimes visitors added to the quantity.

Luckily for me, Johannes also enjoyed cooking and made most of our evening meals. They included a number of different pastas with different meats and sauces that he usually concocted. Nothing like this was cooked by my mum, but I soon got used to the fare, not having eaten pasta as part of a main meal before.

One memory that brings back this type of creation was an evening several months after we had moved into Mount Ararat, the name of the apartment block.

It was about 6:30, and we were having some kind of meatballs with the pasta, which was almost smothered by a chopped tinned tomato-based sauce, washed down by lager.

About halfway through, there was a knock on our entrance door. I could see the outline shadow of a man through the frosted glass door window, and when I got up from the table and answered it, there was a man I had never seen before, standing and bleeding from a number of wounds around but mainly to the top of his head.

His light-coloured, loose sort of jacket, and formerly white shirt as well as the top of his trousers were almost covered in blood.

Very fortunately, we had decided early on to get a first aid box in case of an accident and this and my training in first aid in the mine, came in very useful, enabling me to do a pretty good job of bandaging the man up to stem the bleeding.

The man spoke with near-perfect English but with a strong, East European accent. He did not say very much other than his assailant had hit him over the head with the butt of a revolver. He also refused help from an ambulance, going to the hospital or calling the police, which we found very odd.

Perhaps he was some kind of spy, but what would an eastern bloc country want to spy on South Africa for? The alternative was that he was some sort of gangster, but again, what was he doing here in Johannesburg?

Having finished the bandaging and given the man, whose name was never supplied, a cup of tea, I took him back to the flat next door, so he could clean up better.

I was astonished by the extent of the gore on the walls of the passage when we entered, and also in the kitchen and open bathroom floor as we passed. The passage floor was even worse: it was almost impossible to step on any part of it without standing in his blood. There were even a few red spots on the passage ceiling. (I assumed it was all his, as whoever had done this did not leave a trail to the stairs or lift.)

When we had got ready to go to work the next morning, Johannes and I went to knock on our neighbour's door to see if he was alright but, to our surprise, the door was unlocked and opened easily, after we had first knocked. We just wanted to know if he was alright, but there was no return sound when we called him.

More than that, when we briefly looked around the flat, all signs of life had been removed, and it had been meticulously cleaned from top to bottom, with not a sign of a spot of blood anywhere we looked. Even the few pots and pans looked as if they had been cleaned and carefully put away on the shelves in the kitchen, where I had seen an untidy mess the night before.

At no point during the evening, night or morning had we seen or heard anyone in the flat. Neither had we heard the sound of the lift, which we often did when anyone arrived on or left our floor.

Who on earth can have managed all this cleanup and done it so carefully and quietly, we wondered? Neither Johannes nor I could imagine the victim being able to complete such a feat on his own. Even the ceiling had been wiped spotless.

Johannes had lived in Jo'burg longer than me and already had a few German friends to whom I was introduced.

The longer I stayed with him, the more popular with women he seemed to be. It was amazing just how many fell for him in our time together, and it made me somehow very jealous. Sometimes two or three new admirers arrived in a week! It seemed not to matter to him the age or attractiveness of his partners, but they were mostly in the quite to very attractive categories. In part, it was because his work involved visiting a number of different companies every day that made it easier for him, I thought.

For me, at work, there were no young, fellow copywriters or visualisers, and the only other female in the office who I ever saw regularly was the receptionist who, judging by the ring on her finger, had a permanent relationship and anyway was at least ten years older than me.

It was rare to go out to other locations during the day, and when I did, apart from the odd contact with a receptionist, I never met anyone of my age. I did not get any of Johannes's hand-me-downs either. Poor me! Although I did manage to team up with the occasional female but dared not bring them back to the flat after the first two who instantly seemed to prefer Johannes rather than me.

The consolation was the work I was doing, and seeing the skills of the people I met.

Apart from my slight jealousy as far as Johannes was concerned, he was excellent at managing the household budget. The cost of food and alcohol and anything else bought for the flat was agreed between us and meticulously recorded in his little notebook, right down to the cent. All costs were shared equally, which, for me was an ideal situation.

My primary role was to provide any musical entertainment (television was not available then), but I had all my music on tape, so there was no need to keep getting up to change a record.

Sometimes the conversations were very interesting with people using their own tongue, English or even a range of suitable phrases from English, German and French languages. For me, German was the hardest to follow, but somehow everyone managed to convey what they wanted fairly clearly.

One weekend, Johannes and I invited his two German friends to travel with us to visit the Kruger National Park. This was on a Saturday because it was a long journey—about two hundred miles each way, and I was the only driver, and I wanted some rest before going back to work so needed a break on Sunday after the drive, no accommodation having been found for a stay-over somewhere.

I can't remember what time we left, but we got to the entrance about eleven o'clock.

Initially, I was surprised at the lack of wildlife, but suddenly, we spotted something interesting and stopped to watch what would happen.

About fifty yards away, there was a group of bushes, with two larger trees on either side of a gap where a kudu, facing right as we looked, was nonchalantly munching some grass or low bushes.

Then we saw a leopard slowly entering stage left and almost scraping its body along the ground, obviously looking for a bite to eat.

However, kudu are large antelopes and have long, curly horns and definitely looked quite dangerous themselves.

It took a while to realise that it was being stalked, but when it did, it turned in a flash and put its head down, threatening to attack the leopard with its horns.

For a short while, it waited, both animals eyeing each other. But then the kudu suddenly put its head right down, so that the horns were almost level with the ground, and charged.

The leopard jumped and turned round all in one go and sped off into the distance, while the kudu slowly lifted its head, got up to its full height and tilted its head back slightly, turning it slowly left and right, as though awaiting some kind of applause from an absent, waiting audience, before going back to its feeding once more.

Not much later we went slowly past a large expanse of tall grass, with an upper framework of bushes.

It was really quite boring until we saw a little movement near the centre of the vista. Then, suddenly the grass appeared to move. It was only then that what we could see in the distance was a herd of zebra.

It was quite amazing as once our eyes adjusted to what we were looking at; black-and-white striped shapes became delineated as tens or a hundred or so animals appeared out of the grass that was there before.

I hadn't realised how effective their camouflage could be, as I'd only seen them in a circus before.

We saw other shapes moving through the bush from time to time, but nothing more obvious before we stopped at one of the places that allowed you to get out and buy food and drink.

It was hot, and I for one downed a fair amount of Coke before we left.

Just being in this wilderness was worthwhile and interesting.

Time was getting on when I realised we mi ˙ ˙ ˙ˑt make the 7:00 pm closing time if we continued at the were, so I speeded up a bit, slightly exceed speed limit.

Then I had an urgent need to relieve myself. So I stopped the car near a fairly thick bush to our right and got out. No one else wanted to take the risk of a fine but that was the least of my worries, for I was suddenly aware of something behind me. So I turned my head and looked up at the small cliff where a hungry-looking male lion was staring down at me.

I had no wish to be part of his afternoon meal, and quickly dashed back to the car, pulling myself together as I did so.

With about half an hour of travel still to go, we topped a small hill, and as we were reaching the bottom of the valley, a herd of elephants started to cross the road ahead, possibly led by the matriarch. I didn't look to see if it was female or not as it appeared to be a bit belligerent as it turned, put its head down and began to move towards us. I decided to retreat and drove backwards up the hill we had just come down and carried on down the other side for a bit.

The elephant was nowhere to be seen when I stopped, having been using the mirrors up until then. But we decided to wait a while before trying again.

Strangely, one of my colleagues from work and his girlfriend had experienced the same thing the week before. In his case, the elephants had denied them egress from the park, so they had stayed in their car all night until morning when the gates were opened. It had cost him a fairly high fine.

I didn't want that, so I cautiously drove up and over the hill and past the elephants' crossing point, before speeding up to make the exit in time.

This was not my only encounter with a lion however because, for some reason, I had been invited to come along to a photo shoot for one of my advertisements that was to be taken in a home for retired lions.

After introducing ourselves, a keeper and a girl from the home took us around to one of the lions and let us into his enclosure, which I found somewhat alarming. But we were assured that he spent most of the day just lying in his favourite spot, just in front of a rock.

The keeper left us after the photographer had set up his equipment. "Don't worry, he won't move now he's here," he assured us.

The visualiser started to get a bit fed up as no matter what he did, the lion simply refused to open his mouth.

"Would one of you please go and pull its tail to get him to do something I can use?" he asked.

So I, being closer to the tail than the girl, volunteered and, standing as far away from his body as possible, leant forward and gave the tail a small tug.

At which the lion reluctantly looked up at his audience and opened his mouth.

My visualiser took a couple of quick snaps and put his gear away as soon as he could.

The poor old lion looked irritated at being awoken from his slumber but did nothing more than go back into his previous position but still with his eyes open in case someone annoyed him again.

Just to be sure he wouldn't change his mind, we quickly and quietly left the compound, the girl shutting the gate behind us.

When we got back to the office and the photos developed, the sight was most disappointing. The lion had lost one of its fangs and anyway had a rather ragged coat. So it took a bit of time and effort for the visualiser to restore the image to one of a lion that had all its dentures as well as a smooth coat so that it could be used for a look of strength in the advertisement, though I can't recall the product or service that wanted such an image.

Back at the flat Johannes introduced me to some more friends, another German girl and an attractive Chinese, who I remembered from my short time working as a receptionist with Ipsos Mori.

At Christmas, I had provided a scaled-down Christmas dinner as well as I could for the four of us, who regularly got together and had to make do with sharing a table really designed for two. It was very cosy! How drinks were not spilt was a kind of miracle.

This began a tradition that lasted until I left the country when each of an expanding group would provide a meal from their home country, usually in their own flat. These meals were roughly once a month and later included a Japanese, Toshi Onishi, who I believe was representing Panasonic in South Africa.

I felt sorry for him, as he was not that long in the country when he was invited by Johannes to become one of the gang and had been told by his company to stay in the country for two years before he could get back home and see his wife and children.

When I asked him about his family, he told me that they were safe in their company house and would be looked after by the firm. Apparently, employees of the firm were expected to work for them until they retired, as part of the deal.

I can still remember his turn to contribute to the national meal evening because what he produced was not as good as he wanted.

He was really upset about this, very apologetic, and it sounded as if he was swearing to himself in Japanese between parts of his reason for the poor, in his eyes, standard of cooking.

He explained that he was unable to find a butcher who could cut the beef as thinly as he needed for the fondue style of cooking the meat, which he claimed spoiled the outcome.

Although we all thought it was wonderful, particularly with the accompaniment of the Japanese drink, sake, that he offered us.

Because of the variety of different home languages, most conversations were in English as everyone had a fairly good grasp of it, which was most helpful to me, although the occasional native phrase or expression was added from time to time.

When a particular idiom was explained, it was sometimes used by others in the group, as it was more appropriate to explain a thought or idea using that word or words than those necessary in English. Some sentences had a mixture of French and German expressions incorporated in them, whoever was speaking.

The New Year had just passed, and instead of some fairly bleak work that I had been used to, I was asked to alter an advertisement for a skiing holiday in Austria that someone in our Cape Town office had produced and which had failed abysmally. I had just a day to make it better, as the holidays had to be sold in the next two weeks, and the advertisement was to go in the weekend papers.

The black-and-white background picture of a skier taking a downhill corner in front of a group of fir trees had to remain. Success relied on the copy.

It was both an exciting opportunity and one that scared me a little. But as it had been handed to me in person by our creative director, he obviously had some faith in me. That gave me the confidence to repeat what I had done to get my job in the first place.

I decided that the headline was too obvious and a bit boring, but the body of the explanation was far more promising and interesting.

So I took an unusual chance to take a large portion of the first paragraph in the body of the original advertisement, make it a bit more exciting, and used it as the headline.

When I did this, I was unsure whether the bold print of the heading could be fitted into the space provided. However, the visual artist, who had the job of setting the type and sizes to be used, assured me that it was quite alright.

He did a great job, I thought, and so to my delight and relief did the creative director despite the fact that my only real contribution was to simplify and make minor changes to the copy that had been written in the Cape Town office.

On Sunday, I went out and bought a copy of the paper to see what it looked like on the page and was pleased to see that it stood out from the competition, as it was so different to the norm.

The client was delighted too, according to our CD, as he came around to me on Tuesday to tell me that all the holidays were already sold out, just one day later.

I had another piece of luck later in January. I was sitting with nothing to do one morning when a senior female colleague, who I only met once regarding work, came into my little cubicle and asked if I would take over her task.

I was astonished when I saw the record she also had with her: it was Simon and Garfunkel's 'Bridge over troubled water' album that she said was horrible.

I couldn't believe it, as I liked their work, and it was just the opportunity that I was waiting for.

I can still remember going into the large photo studio and sitting on a wooden chair to listen to both sides of it, slightly marred by the fairly cheap player and poor acoustics, as there was a bit of an echo. The immediate effect it had reminded me of my first hearing of Sergeant Pepper's Lonely Hearts Club Band.

If I didn't believe her before, I certainly couldn't afterwards as I was so excited by it.

There was nothing in the brief about what the client might want, other than it was to be a half-page newspaper ad.

So I wrote something like, 'This must be the best ever album in the world'. The exact wording I used could be different, as I must have written a dozen or more slogans of the sort before opting for the one that proved to be true, judging by its worldwide sales.

CBS Records were delighted and this success led to me being the copywriter they asked for to do all their advertising thereafter—and they gave me the album that I had written the copy for, which I still have in my collection.

I did a few job adverts for them too because they thought, as I was still young, I might use such awful phrases, as I think now, as 'wanted—a swinging, hip chick to be secretary for …' etcetera.

I also wrote radio scripts for LPs, such as *Fill Your Head with Rock*, that was the first double album of its kind to contain tracks from a number of bands and artists like Blood Sweat & Tears, Bob Dylan, Janice Joplin and Chicago.

The Greatest Rock Album You'll Ever Want was the repeated message in the Sunday newspapers in the bottom right corner of six pages of the leisure sections.

The only drawback of writing radio scripts was going to the studio to approve the recordings.

Walking along Commissioner Street in the sunshine was pleasant enough, but the booth that the sound recordist worked in was about fifteen to twenty feet wide, and apart from the door to the studio on the left and a glass screen, so one could see the studio itself, the wall was covered with large loudspeakers that the technician had just about as loud as they could go.

It meant that during the quarter-mile walk back to the office I heard nothing from the six lanes of traffic passing me.

However, there was one recording when only a voice was being used, so the sound was more reasonable.

On that occasion, I experienced the strangest coincidences possible for, after about a hundred yards I bumped into someone from my village in Kent. He worked for SAS, the Scandinavian Airlines company, and was here on business. We had a brief chat, then I walked on another hundred or so yards, and coming towards me was the son of the pub at the bottom of the main road, again from Staplehurst. He was simply on holiday.

Six thousand miles from home, and I meet one three hundred and fiftieth of the population of the village then!

While thinking about odd things happening when I went to the studio, there was another time one morning I saw what

I guessed was an old farm lorry coming down Commissioner Street as I was crossing one of the intersections.

What made it stand out as such was that it looked as if it had just come back from a distant desert war twenty or thirty years earlier, so unusual was its light tan exterior and more or less horizontal driving wheel with near vertical twin rectangular glass windscreens.

Inside was a grey-haired elderly driver with a round wired spectacle and even a clay pipe in his mouth and, I guessed, his wife in an old-fashioned dress that made it look as though she had dressed for a special occasion, which this presumably rare visit to the city probably was.

Having got into the middle of the traffic light-controlled crossroad, he turned right into what he must have assumed was an open road with no cars on it.

Unfortunately, the traffic lights further in front of him turned green as he made the turn. His eyes seemed to bulge and pop out, and his jaw dropped, as did his pipe, when he saw, coming towards him a solid stream of cars four lanes wide.

He looked completely puzzled by the sight, and his wife held a hand to her mouth when she also sensed potential disaster. The driver simply continue his lorry chugging slowly along, as the opposing cars had to slow and divert past him.

At last, he reached the next set of lights. There he just managed to turn left and get behind the last of the cars going from right to left in front of him, before the next set of cars in front of him were released by the lights.

It looked as if he had never travelled into the city for many years. It was yet another caricature of a scene that could have been in a black-and-white comedy film from the thirties. It certainly made me astonished at first, and then chuckle to myself as I relived the scene over and over again as I walked on to my destination, there to tell the technician what I had seen and see him rock in his seat with laughter at the story.

About three years later, when I saw the Bond film, Live and Let Die, I wondered if the screenwriter for that film had been in Jo'burg and seen what I had then and incorporated it for the time when Bond was in a speedboat being chased on the road by US police.

Fortunately, nothing like that happened during the recording, and as it was a simple voice-over and didn't require any fancy acting, I was able to depart quite quickly.

A pleasant memory from the hot summer days was an almost regular rainstorm at about 4:00 pm that only lasted a short time but cooled and cleared the atmosphere nicely before the walk home from work around half past.

In late July, our representative to CBS came into my little office and asked if I would like to see Percy Sledge at the Empire Theatre this coming Friday. Of course, I said yes.

When I got there, the rep and a couple of others from Lindsay-Smithers were already seated in the front row of the circle.

Despite images of his little band being shown on the publicity, Percy Sledge was on his own in front of a light red curtain the whole night.

As his accompanying music appeared to be coming from behind him, I assume that his band was there and could make out his signals through the curtain in front of them. He certainly made an odd gesture or more while he was on stage, probably to indicate the start of the next set of numbers.

It was certainly very odd to see the artist on his own throughout the performance when he sang all of his hits and most popular songs. It is unlikely that his backing was recorded back in 1970, but if it wasn't, the programme was very slick.

Another odd thing that I did not realise at first was that the audience was all white, while the artist was black. I wondered why it was that Percy Sledge had agreed to this before embarking on his tour.

CBS seemed to like what I did for them as, shortly after that event, I began to be asked to go to their offices after our Friday afternoon functions at our offices.

Then whoever the contact was would play some of their future releases, imported from the States, for the rep and I to comment on—and to enjoy even more liquor with him—then to imbibe a bit more with a meal at their disco, and to stay on if I wanted, with further drinks on the house.

It was all very nice but a bit too much every Friday so, after the first couple of evenings, I declined any more nights at the disco because Friday evenings in the flat were usually more entertaining—and I preferred the simple but tasty meals that Johannes made much more, along with the conversation.

I'm not sure why but one afternoon I had gone on my own somewhere out of Jo'burg, but I do remember the return journey in the evening through some hills before I got into Jo'burg. This trip might have been earlier, and I may be remembering one of my market research days rather than something to do with advertising.

Anyway, the sun had gone down, and I was approaching a wooded area. Still a mile or so away I could see hundreds of lightning flashes, but it was only when I got much closer that

I realised that the thunderstorm seemed to be concentrating all its effort on the forest of what appeared to be dry autumnal trees.

Then I was in the thick of it, the road snaking between the trees that were constantly being struck by lightning, accompanied by a loud crackling noise but at least making the road easy to see. The noise must have been quite loud to be heard, even if I did have the car windows open, I was surprised that the trees didn't immediately catch fire, though the flashes were stripping small lengths of burning bark as the trees were struck.

Certainly, there was a strong smell of wood burning, but instead of yellow light, the forest near the ground was cast in a grey-blue light, as though lit by neon lights rather than fire.

Suddenly, the trees and storm stopped, and at last, I could see the street lights of Jo'burg below me, and the rest of my journey was without incident.

It was not quite the same a few nights later when I went out onto our balcony with a newspaper in my hand to show Johannes an advertisement I had written. He was already sitting and reading a magazine.

It was surprising because the light that made reading possible was coming from the lightning storms in every direction around the hills circling the city. It was almost as good as daylight, perhaps because it was a white light that gave a good contrast between the slightly off-white of the paper and the black of the ink.

I also remember travelling back from a journey a group of four of us made one Sunday. We set off with no particular plan, just a trip to look at the countryside towards Durban. It can't have been that exceptional because the only part I can recall was stopping the car during our return journey, just after a bridge to have a picnic under some trees by a river.

Johannes and I got a basket of food and drink, together with a blanket to sit on, and took them down the river bank, where we could see a nice place to sit.

But as we were about to put them down, and before the two girls who had come with us arrived, we quickly picked up our things because emerging from the river with a hungry look in its eyes was a crocodile.

So I just drove off to find a spot, away from the river, to stop for the picnic that we now really hungered for.

Other than this, there were no alarms, and we got back to Jo'burg safely.

Back at Lyndsey-Smithers, one morning I heard a voice from over the connecting wall in our room. It was one of our senior copywriters who was calling to ask if her slogan cum heading was suitable for a new product from Kimberly Clark, among other things a manufacturer of toilet tissues.

Coincidentally, when I was working for Ipsos Mori, I was assigned to the survey that they were doing for the tissue maker, but then I was unaware that this was their client.

The survey was designed to find out which would be the most popular design, for a new shape of a box that they wanted to put on the market. There were two exterior options for the square box; one was black with coloured dots on it that resembled a dice, and the other was made oblong for ease of extraction of the tissues inside, and the other box had a pale colour background and a floral foreground.

The dice had strong, bright colours the same as the colour of the tissues it contained, and the floral version had light shades that also corresponded with the tissues inside.

Just from my research, I could see the overwhelming popularity of the black dice.

This product came towards the end of the pop art period, so it was much more acceptable than possibly it would have been in the early Sixties, particularly as it was a common sort of sculpture that was well known, and largely reminiscent of childhood games, with just the difference of the vibrant colours on its exterior.

Everyone I interviewed could imagine this box being kept anywhere, like in the office, in a bathroom, or in any room in the house. It would be reasonably acceptable to men as well as women.

When I popped around to look at my colleagues' work I could see at once that it was the same dice-like box that I had asked people about several months before.

My colleague explained that South Africa was to be the company's test market for the novel shape, so the advertising had to be especially good.

The slogan she was so pleased with was, 'Nice 'n' Dicey'.

"That's really wonderful!" I remember exclaiming. "It fits perfectly with the box and what the public feel about it."

She queried how I knew that, and I explained my opinion research.

"Thank you." She got up with a broad smile and probably would have attempted to dance with me if there had been enough room.

So 'Nice 'n' Dicey' it was to be. What was particularly good about it was the fact that it could be understood and used on the radio to back up the cinema and press advertising.

The result was that this new tissue box had taken nearly 80% of the whole tissue market within two months.

This was too much to last, so Kimberly Clark decided to start selling the floral design as well, thus making it hard for the competition to compete. The combination certainly ensured that the mass of their sales almost completely destroyed their competition.

I was also involved in, for me, a very exciting opportunity not long after my colleague's greatest triumph.

When I heard the name of the client, South Africa Rubber Manufacturing Company, my thoughts were anything but excited, but when it was explained to me, and the visual artist assigned to work with me, what it entailed, it was an opportunity above any I could have wished for.

Apart from anything else, this was the visual artist's first important assignment, and more than that, he was responsible for much of the Sea of Holes sequence in the Beatle's Yellow Submarine film.

Together, the newies had to advertise a novel ice tray and create a logo for a new branch of the firm.

Up until now, the Rubber Manufacturing Company was known for three main types of products: V-belts for car fans, industrial rubber belts for transporting stone or ingredients like powders in industrial situations and condoms.

The new product was based on a light blue kind of rubber that had been produced in error—someone had mixed the rubber for another type of product incorrectly. But, before throwing it away, someone suggested that it could be used in an ice tray because it was strong enough to keep its shape but had a shiny surface and became fairly elastic when pressed with a finger.

All it needed was a metal bar to keep it rigid when putting water in it, and small holes between the rectangular compartments for ice to be kept in place until the cubes were wanted when they would break as the cube was pressed out of its temporary home.

This was much better than the metal trays against which it would be competing. The metal trays often froze to the extent that breaking the ice cubes out of them was difficult, if not dangerous. Certainly, I and some people I knew, had received cut fingers or other little injuries when using them.

The actual advertisement was created during discussions together.

The image was pretty obvious: originally with a couple of thumbs and fingers on either side of the tray, pushing it up and cubes flying in the air, then the partial hands were removed and just the tray with a simple metal bar below and cubes flying out was used.

A copy was almost unnecessary: just 'POP-IT' in large 3-D type curving round in an arc above the exploding cubes, and below, "The simply safe way to get ice cubes"—what more was needed?

The only thing left was to create a suitable name and logo for the new, domestic product part of the company; South African Rubber Manufacturing Company Limited.

Using its initials alone or the full name would be meaningless to the general public and could even detract from the appeal of the image. It was much too much of a mouthful, and would hardly be suitable for inclusion in the market they were entering, especially as the only 'domestic' type of product that they already made was a condom, and mixing that with an ice cube tray was not an image they would want, I thought.

So, what did the ad and company need? Something appealing that would indicate reliability, quality and just a hint of youthfulness and novelty.

It didn't take long to think of Switzerland, the land of high-quality and reliable watches that everyone would recognise. But what sort of symbol could represent the idea?

The name came to me almost as soon as the image was established in our minds: Heidi Products of course, with my artist colleague quickly sketching a cartoon kind of milkmaid in traditional costume, a white hat, looking a bit like a yacht and sail together, and the largely red typical imaginary Swiss dress.

The sketch was soon made sharper and coloured in. Somehow he managed to make it look welcoming and warm, with a hint of quality.

It is really fascinating to see how our discussions were so simply and cleverly turned into this trade mark by my colleague.

When we showed him the finished advertisement, as we saw it, our representative to the company just said, "Wow, that's great."

The company hierarchy later awarded it Ad of the Month, and we were told that SARMC were delighted with the whole concept.

Back home, Johannes and I were delighted to be asked one day to have a meal at our Chinese friend's house.

Like the Japanese Toshi Inishi, Chinese people were considered Honorary Whites in South Africa, so I knew that although they must almost certainly live in an area where other Chinese lived, it would be reasonably close and within Johannesburg.

Actually, it was on the outskirts but still easy to get to simply by walking, which was fortunate as there was quite a lot to drink during the meal.

It is a shame that I can't remember the family's or our friend's name because her mother was wonderfully welcoming when we arrived just before seven in the evening.

The meal was something special, and could well have been for a birthday, but again I can't remember, but I still have a feeling of guilt associated with images of the repast, so possibly it was.

The meal started soon after we arrived, with our female friend seated between us for the purposes of translation: both the conversation and the rules associated with the meal.

The meal itself was very different to any I had experienced before although I don't remember exactly what we had though it consisted of many different courses and took until after ten o'clock to come to an end.

Each course was quite small and accompanied by a different alcoholic drink each time, also in a small glass. Nevertheless, there was always enough time for another sip and a bit of chat before the next course came along.

The only real problem was getting used to manipulating the food using chopsticks for the first time, in such a way that it arrived safely in one's mouth rather than on the table cloth or lap.

After the repast, we were shown to the entertainment area, where mahjong was being played. Unfortunately, it was impossible to grasp the rules or understand what gambit might be being played, so a couple of others retired to a lounge to continue chatting until, a little after midnight, we said our thanks and goodbyes to our hosts, who were still enjoying their game.

This encounter led to yet another invitation to a rather special event.

In this case, it was a christening that took place in a large room with a bar in it. It was not possible to guess exactly what the place was used for normally, but a shorter meal was provided before and after the christening ceremony itself.

Unfortunately, this was also very hard to follow, being conducted in Chinese, but we felt very honoured to have been asked to such an occasion, where there were so many relatives and Chinese friends of the baby's family, but no one else who was not Chinese.

This time, we knew the purpose of the event, and Johannes and I subscribed to a silver rattle, or something similar, that we presented to the parents. I think they were a bit surprised that we had thought to give a christening present.

Fortunately, we sat with people we knew, who were kind enough to explain what was going on, and also used English most of the night.

Returning to my work, there were infrequent late nights when I was required to check that an advertisement that I had written had the right typeface, and any illustration correctly placed within the block that would be used for printing the newspaper that night.

Sometimes it meant sitting around drinking coffee for a couple of hours, and only leaving around midnight. It wasn't always just sitting, as the restroom had a darts board. Using it by myself was not much fun, but often there was someone from the print room who was waiting until he could do his bit. So we would while away the time together.

One night I was with a fellow copywriter when one of the printers came in to ask if we would like to make up a team from Lindsay-Smithers to take on the printers team.

I only remember playing against them a couple of times, and the sessions only lasted an hour or two. We were playing after work and the printers before they started theirs, but I think it helped ensure that the work we sent them was set up carefully.

Once again I was given the task of writing an advertisement for CBS. This was again a radio script for *Fill Your Head with Rock*—a compilation LP with artists like Blood, Sweat and Tears, Santana and Chicago on it.

I duly put together all the in words I could together with a few named examples for a Lorenzo Marques DJ to read out. I had to make a couple of adjustments in the studio because I had not been told which excerpts from the album CBS wanted in the background.

I thought it was my worst effort, but apparently, CBS really liked it and their sales were very good. I even now play some of the tracks sometimes.

Strangely, when I walked back to the office I bumped into a former near neighbour of ours from Staplehurst who worked for SAS Scandinavian Airlines and was on business in Jo'burg. We just had a brief chat and went our own ways but not a couple of hundred yards further on I bumped into the son of the landlord at the Railway Tavern, opposite the road into the station at Staplehurst. He was just on holiday but was in a hurry to catch a train or coach—I can't remember which, so apart from a brief exchange of greetings and telling each other why we were there, it was just an amazing surprise.

How odd, I thought to myself, meeting two adults out of about eight hundred living in our village at that time, and some six thousand miles away. What were the chances of doing that, I wondered, as I continued back to work?

I mentioned before about me and other staff at the agency being used as a free model for the agency. Nobody minded doing this because we were all well paid, and it was often an interesting experience, or just a change, to be taken away from our normal work for a half hour or more. They also meant that often we could be seen in the press to show off to our friends.

For instance, although a new boy copywriter at twenty-two, I was earning one and a half times more than I did working underground, and that was considered a well-paid job. My salary just in my first year of being a surveyor was 15% more than my dad's when he died, and he held a fairly senior position in the highways department of Kent County Council.

Anyway, when I got back to the office eight of us, a mixture of male and female: the capacity for the Toyota Combi for which we were doing the advert, were taken into a square not far from our office.

There we found our cameraman, a ladder for him to stand on and a number of spotlights shining on us and the combi, despite it being a sunny day.

We were ushered into the line-up our photographer wanted and had to wait for a while before he was satisfied that the picture would be as the creative team wanted.

During this wait, I was amazed as I looked at all the office blocks surrounding the square, to see hundreds of women looking out of almost all the windows, trying to get a good look at the sudden arrival of celebrities in the lights, some of them waving it seemed to be sure that we saw them.

Oh! Didn't I feel good as I was sure that at least a couple of very attractive girls nearby were waving and smiling, just at me? Unfortunately, nothing came of it as we were whisked away as soon as the shoot finished.

And anyway, I could see their sudden disappearance as their bosses found out what the disturbance was and quickly shooed them back to their desks to continue typing. Well, at least I'd be in the papers again. Not that that did much good for my personal life either.

Not long after this, Toyota was once more involved with my life.

I was busy working away on the promotion leaflet for a new five-star hotel that was being built in Johannesburg that I mentioned earlier when one of our reps almost charged into my office.

He seemed a little out of breath, as he got out the question, "Would you be able to drive a car tonight?"

I grunted something really useful like, "Huh?"

Then, he rapidly explained that the person who was supposed to drive the new Toyota Corolla back to the garage, after its demonstration at the Kyalami Circuit, has gone down sick, and they need someone to do this for them.

It seemed a bit weird that there was no one else from Toyota, or their main showroom in Johannesburg, who could do the job. But I happily agreed, even though I didn't know Johannesburg very well, let alone where the racing circuit was and had never been to the outlet in the outskirts of Jo'burg either.

Originally, the rep was going to take me to the dealership, but this changed about half an hour before we were due to leave.

The rep rushed into my room again and told me the directions to the dealership, and that I should get there by seven.

I was allowed to leave work a bit early so that I could have my evening meal, change and drive my mini to the garage in good time.

This I did.

When I got there, it took a while to find whoever it was in charge. Then, when I did and explained who I was and what I was expecting to do, he told me that one of the groups going from the garage would give me a lift to the Grand Prix circuit.

We waited around for about half an hour for no apparent reason.

Then the order to go was announced and my driver came to invite me to his car.

The drive didn't take very long, but I was not very clear about the route, sitting as I was in the back seat of the car.

Arriving in Kyalami, I looked around to find who was now in charge of the proceedings.

When I did, and told him why I was there, he told me, "You really need not have bothered, someone else is going to drive the Corolla back."

I explained that my car was at the dealership, but he told me not to worry as someone else would take me home. "Just enjoy yourself—all the drinks and whatever you want to eat is on the house."

Because I had expected to drive the Corolla and my mini at the end of the evening, I had prepared myself not to have a drink that evening, but now I was free to indulge myself for the next few hours.

For whatever reason, our rep was nowhere to be seen, and everyone else was busy talking to people they already knew.

I took a stroll outside to have a bit of a look around, returning to the main gathering at about 9:30. I was surprised to see how much of the room had cleared – now there were less than twenty.

Someone I didn't know came up to me.

"I believe you were told that someone else was taking the car back, but he suddenly had to leave, so now you will have to drive it."

I remember the sudden shock I felt. I'm just twenty-three, don't know anyone here, have no idea about the route back to the dealership and I'm not very sober, and I have to drive home after that. These thoughts circled in my mind while I was thinking about how I might get out of it.

What could I do? It seemed that everything had been decided for me, without anyone thinking to say something when they had learnt their driver was no longer available. It was only later that I wondered how many people in the crowd were actually sober enough to drive home.

Without saying any more, or even asking if it was alright, this third man ushered me to the brand-new Corolla: the only one in South Africa at the time, and that was due to be taken down to Cape Town for demonstration the next day.

"Here are the keys," he said handing them to me. A moment later I realised I did not know how to get out of the race track. I looked back and called, but the door we had come out by was closed and the light switched off, and I had no idea where he had gone.

I left abandoned. Even more so as I had to work out how and where the car's essentials, such as the light switch or gear lever, were and where the gears were. By the time I had found these things out, I discovered that everyone else had gone. The area where all the private cars were parked was on the other side of the building and was empty when I found my way past the grandstand. Just how would I find my way out and to the dealership I wondered.

All I knew was the exit number on the motorway that I needed to take to get to the nearby garage but not how to get to the motorway from Kyalami.

I just guessed what general direction to take, driving as cautiously as I could along a metalled road.

Then, over to my left, I saw lights of fast-moving cars almost parallel to the road I was on.

Suddenly, I came upon a turning to my left that I thought might take me to the rushing lights, but this was a dirt road. *But it must get me to the motorway,* I thought. As I was thinking this, there was a tight left-hand corner, with a high sandy side to it. So high that I did not see a lone rock, about a foot or so high, on the road in front of me.

I had no time to brake completely and hit it.

When I got out of the car to check the damage, I could feel the front mudguard being pushed back towards the wheel. Of course, I moved the fairly heavy rock out of the way, and then found, to my good fortune, I was able to pull the mudguard clear of the tyre, and nearly how it should normally look—I hoped.

I went on, lights on the motorway at least in the same direction I was going.

The next thing I remember seeing was a sign for the motorway as I went up a bridge.

This would be the first experience I had of driving onto one in the dark.

It was soon very clear that my lack of knowledge had led me down the wrong way: I was going in the right direction but on the wrong side of the road! As I suddenly discovered when I joined the motorway.

Luckily for me, there were no other traffic around or coming towards me, and no central barrier, so I was able to cross over the kerbs and get on the right side of the motorway without endangering me or anyone else.

Not long afterwards I saw the exit sign I needed and left the motorway. Fortunately, I recognised the road and found the garage without difficulty.

It was nearly empty—just a couple of people waiting for the car, to ready it for its onward journey the next morning. When they saw what had happened, there was some muttering that I could hear but ignored. I told them what had happened before I left the race track and how I had managed to damage the front wing. Then left as soon as I could.

The next day I had a very unhappy boss asking for me. However, he soon changed what he thought after his phone call from the garage when he heard my version of exactly what had transpired the day before.

Having checked back with our rep, and the manager of the showroom, he came to my room to apologise and to tell me that he was very angry with the Toyota dealership, who admitted exactly what had happened to put me in the position I had found myself.

Towards the end of 1970, two things happened that made me consider my future in South Africa.

The first was a government announcement that anyone, under twenty-five, who had a visa to work in South Africa and had stayed for five years, could be called up for military service. As I understood it, you did not have to be a citizen with a South African passport to be enlisted.

The second was something I heard being discussed about a partner agency in London that, apparently, had a kind of operational agreement that organisations like South African Airways could have some business passed on to them through ourselves, and likewise the reverse was true for some other businesses they had.

This meant that the same kind of format and graphics would be used when a product or service was being advertised at much the same time in both countries.

Of course, there would need to be modifications to the ads that had originally been produced in the initiating country as, obviously, such things as a contact address or some kind of local symbol or scenery, might be out of place in the second country.

This started an idea in my head that it might be an opportunity for me to go back and learn how to create television advertisements if I could get an arrangement with our partner organisation to have a job there.

South Africa did not have television then, so I might be in more demand if I could later return to SA with the knowledge that would be required to write TV advertisements.

Of course, there were advertisements screened at cinemas and drive-ins, but these were rarely of the home-produced variety because of their usual length and the local cost of making them, as well as the comparatively small audience able to see them. (As far as I was aware, film audiences were exclusively white; on the other hand, there would be nothing to stop black people from having a TV at home if they could afford it, and the ads would be seen by a much larger white and honorary white audience when not limited to cinemas.)

As my time in SA was approaching this new compulsory, if requested, call-up I did not wish to lose three years or however long doing it, having only comparatively recently learnt my current trade.

So I tentatively asked if some arrangement for a kind of transfer could be made to our partner company in London, should I be called up or simply want to go soon, for the training and expertise that I would acquire if I could learn how to do TV ads.

At this time, South Africa was preparing to start television transmission, so I thought working in the UK for a while would give me an advantage if I returned.

Anyway, I let that rest for a while.

During the weekend following, our flat was very quiet for a change, as everyone we knew was away on holiday or for some other reason. So instead of sitting around drinking, on Saturday we decided to have a walk around some parts of Jo'burg that we had never seen.

We headed south of Commissioner Street and along a parallel road just looking to see what it was like.

Actually, it was rather boring, with main blocks of offices, just like Commissioner Street it seemed but after a while the height of the buildings began to change, though I can't remember much about them until we came to a glass-fronted café.

By now, we were getting a bit thirsty from walking in the heat, so we looked in and saw some cheap tables and chairs and two black men. One was behind the light-blue/grey-fronted bar, and the other was at one end chatting with him.

We had only taken a few steps when a shout came from the man behind the counter.

"You can't come in here—get out!" he shouted.

We were totally bemused. Never had we been refused by anyone of colour.

"We just want to get a drink," Johannes replied.

"Get out, you're not allowed in here."

I noticed a Coke can dispenser against the yellow-painted wall to our left.

"Can we just get a can from here?" I asked, waving my hand towards it. "We'll get straight out afterwards."

The man relented and just said, "Get a couple of cans if you want and then get straight out."

Obviously, our general politeness had some benefit. *Perhaps,* I thought to myself, *he must be used to white men shouting at him and telling him what to do.* We hadn't realised that we were in a black quarter, or so it seemed in this somewhat run-down area.

Perhaps this is the only sort of place that black people working in the city could go for a break I wondered.

Anyway, we quickly got our drinks and called out our 'Thank yous' as we left.

I looked back and saw a little smile on the barman's face as I went out of the door, and back into the heat of the day.

This encounter had been a complete surprise to us. I don't know why, but of course, our lives were not normally constrained like black peoples were. (With the exception of the honorary whites—Chinese and Japanese people.) So we naturally thought we could go anywhere, except in black townships. What a strange world!

After that, we decided to wend our way back to our flat through the roads we knew. It was all a bit of a waste of time, but we did see another part of South Africa, which made both of us think a bit.

Now it was my turn to think very carefully about what I should do. I could stay in Jo'burg and enjoy what I considered a fairly easy and interesting job but with the risk of being called up to the army.

Of course, the change that the government had made had only just started to be implemented, and I had not heard of anyone being called up, but should I risk it?

That last thought, even though periods in the army were broken up into three, I was told, and that my job had to be retained, but that prospect was not what I wanted at all.

So I decided to check whether my thought about getting a job at our partner agency was a real possibility. So, first thing on Monday morning at the start of November I asked our creative director (also his role on the company's board) whether he had heard anything.

I also wanted to make sure that I gave enough notice, as time was running out and there was a lot to be arranged if I was to leave.

I was pleasantly surprised when he told me that he had received a letter saying that there was a place for me if I wanted to take it up.

I answered, "In one way, I don't want to go, as I so enjoy it here. But if there is a chance to gain an understanding of TV advertising, and how it can be approached from a copywriter's point of view, I would like to think there could be a place back here for me if one was available."

He said that he could not give me a definite response to that, but of course, they would be happy to take me back. "I suppose you would want more money then," he said as he grinned at me. "When would you like to leave?"

"It has to be before the Tenth of December, but I will let you know when I will be able to travel."

(I had already managed to contact my brother, who had agreed to put me up and collect me when I arrived back in England though, at that stage, I could not tell him where and when I would arrive.)

At lunchtime, I went to a travel agency, thinking that it would be best to go by boat, as I had more to carry than when I travelled to South Africa when my trunk was sent before me.

I found out that Canberra was sailing from Cape Town on the Third of December, a Thursday, almost exactly five years from when I left England. To catch it, I needed to leave Jo'burg by the overnight train on Tuesday the First, only a couple of weeks away.

Returning to work, I immediately went to the CD again and told him about my plans, and why I needed to go then.

Despite the fairly short notice, he told me that he understood and would get everything ready. Money was particularly important as the journey by boat was quite expensive, and just at this moment, I did not have enough.

I had tried to suppress it, but the feeling of guilt that I had about the white lie that I had told him; that I had received notice of my call-up, grew to its peak now, as I also began to realise the effect my move might make: both to the ad agency, who would now need a replacement, as all copywriters seemed incredibly busy, and to Johannes because of the short notice although Johannes was a very good planner, and I thought, *he would manage all right.*

However, I also had to sell my car. Fortunately, I managed to do this quite quickly and did not lose too much money compared with its cost. With what I had, it was just enough to pay the travel costs, including one night in a hotel in Cape Town.

As soon as I got back to the flat, I told Johannes when I would be leaving. I had not thought then, about the fact that he would now be responsible for the full cost of the flat, as I was too absorbed in my plans, including what I could manage to take and, perhaps, leave behind. Also, I kept thinking whether this really was the right thing to do but, remembering the suddenness that I had left the mine, what would it really matter? After all, I did have the promise of a job to go to.

My mind seemed to be in a terrible mess again, and I still had much to do.

There were a couple of jobs I still had to finish, but I could not put my mind fully on those, and no magical appearance of words seemed to appear the way they used to.

Of course, Johannes already knew I would be leaving soon, so I thought that a good planner like him would already have made some kind of arrangement.

I suddenly remembered that I would have to get my last salary into the bank and have time to change it into pounds both for the journey to Canberra and for when I was back in England. So, before my final day and after talking to my boss, he arranged for the payment to be a few days before my last working day. Just the cost of the trip to Canberra cost £146 in 1970, about 10% of my annual salary then.

It meant that I had to find time to get to my bank, close my account and get the money I needed in both Rands and pounds at the same time. I felt like I was coming and going at the same time. Just what would I forget, I wondered.

I had tickets for the overnight train on Tuesday that gave me an afternoon in Cape Town, after booking into the hotel, to have a little sunbathe on the sand.

By the end of the last weekend in Jo'burg, I had everything I needed to pack away and put in my trunk or case ready for my journey.

I left the Revox and some tapes for Johannes, as well as the radiogram I had somehow managed to fit in my mini when I left Welkom, as there was certainly no space left in the trunk for that, after my piles of records that I desperately wanted to keep, as well as all the other things that I would not need on the boat.

My! My trunk was heavy! The thought of carrying my suitcase and my trunk to and from the train, then to the hotel and then onto the boat, was daunting. I just hoped that there would be some assistance to hand when had to transfer from taxi to train, to taxi again and on to the hotel, then from there to customs and the boat.

On Saturday, there was a farewell meal and drinks for me with all our friends.

It was both a sad day and one when my brain seemed to be arguing with itself whether this really was a good idea. Finally, opting for the thought that everything was now arranged, I really could not go back.

Nevertheless, my stomach still managed the odd turn before I began the actual departure: thinking of my friends and colleagues at work who were almost a family to me by now, and how much I would miss them, and the wonderful work I had been doing. Would it be the same in England, I wondered.

When I left England I was excited and saw a wonderful future in front of me, now I felt somehow that I was diving into the abyss. Virtually, everything had been planned for me when I left home, and I had some idea of what I would expect, but now everything was up to me, and I was not that certain where I would be living.

I had managed to contact my brother to tell him when I would arrive in Southampton, and he had assured me that his wife, Janet, would collect me from the boat and that I could stay with them if I wanted.

But for how long, I asked myself, or would I go back to live with my mum? Much depended on my job in London.

I was very sad on the Saturday evening of the farewell meal, as I was leaving an interesting bunch of friends.

Sleeping that night was difficult, as I fretted about my having used a white lie to leave South Africa, as I had not had notification of a call-up that I had used as an excuse for returning to the UK. I was also worried about my job in London as, apart from knowing its address I wasn't sure what I should do to contact the agency.

On Monday, I had to travel a thousand miles to Cape Town.

Somehow I managed to get everything together that I needed: loose change and notes, passport, the note of the hotel I was to stay in overnight on Tuesday, and the train and boat tickets, and hope that the plans in my head would go smoothly.

Just taking my suitcase and very heavy trunk downstairs and into the taxi was bad enough, but the reverse action to unload and then get to the right platform with my baggage was a bit of a chore, but I managed it alright, depositing my trunk in the guard's van and taking my suitcase to my sleeping compartment for the twenty-five-hour journey.

The day travelling is a blur as it was quite boring looking out at the bland countryside. I did manage some conversation with the others in the sleeper, but what was said, and the meals we had I simply can't recall.

The only thing that I can still remember I was stopping in the dark night, waking in some sort of shed with its lights showing a few adjacent lines with empty metal trucks on them, that I could see by looking out of the window from my upper bunk.

The only other things before I fell asleep again, were of our train being shunted and banging into something as it went backwards. Then, after staying still for some time, we moved very slowly forward.

I can't remember the countryside or houses going by before finally stopping at our destination either.

Everything went smoothly when I got to Cape Town, but I was by no means the first to get a taxi, so I rolled up later than I had expected at the hotel.

Nevertheless, I had enough time to get out my swimming trunks and take a towel to have a little swim and an hour or two sunbathing on a nearby otherwise deserted sandy beach.

I regretted sunbathing the next morning when getting up and putting on my shoes, as the tops of my feet were burnt and sore.

Otherwise, the next thing I recall is entering the side of the Canberra, and being guided to a lower deck cabin near the rear stairway.

Luckily, although made for two, I was the only inhabitant for the whole of my journey. At least it had a porthole, but it was only just above the sea, and around head height, so there was not much of a view.

It was also only two decks up to where the restaurant was, so not too badly placed for my meals. Higher up was a bar and a deck to walk around and above all else a pool, disco and room to play ping-pong.

Playing table tennis was a bit difficult at times, as the room used was on the top deck and the table was placed port to starboard so, when the sea was a bit rough, the ship kind of lurched (because of the effect of the stabilisers) so sometimes a ball aimed at the far side of the table would go over the top, or land in its middle, when a quick adjustment was needed by the receiver if he was to return the ball.

Anyway, it was all good fun, as was the disco, where I discovered that there were slightly more girls than young men. Consequently, a few free partners—not like in Welkom.

I soon teamed up with a very nice girl, who immediately explained her situation: that she was travelling back to England to be with her fiancé and thus didn't want to have matters go too far but did want the regular company to chat sometimes but still enjoy a bit of intimacy.

That suited me well enough as she was very pleasant company, and I wasn't keen on becoming too close with anyone, as I wasn't sure where I would be living in the UK, and hoped I would find a partner near where I might end up.

Lounging on the deck in the sunshine or having a short swim were my only other activities. Really, I just wanted a relaxing time.

En route to Madeira, we crossed the equator and those who had not done so before took part in the crossing-the-line ceremony in recognition of Neptune.

I didn't realise what was going on until I heard a bit of a noise coming from the top deck, where I found a crowd of people looking down on the swimming pool, where the uninitiated were ceremoniously dunked in the pool one by one, much to the enjoyment of those not taking part.

It was a few days more before we arrived one morning at Madeira and moored on the outer quay at its capital, Funchal.

There were a couple of coach trips laid on for us, and I went on one that took us south and up to a cliff that the guide said was a thousand feet high. Then we were dropped in the centre of Funchal for a wander around before re-embarking.

It was there that I bought an airmail copy of the Daily Telegraph—at last, a decent paper to read and do the crosswords.

I waited until I was back on board before I read through the paper.

It was then I had a terrible shock. On the business pages was an article about the ad agency that I was supposed to be joining. It said that the agency had been taken over by an American company and that half its staff had been sacked and replaced by others from the States.

Would I have the promised job? How could I find out? I would just have to wait until I was back in England I supposed.

I decided that, for now, I would just enjoy myself as much as I could, so my worries could be set aside.

Life on board went on in much the same way as we sailed on to Lisbon, where we anchored somewhere off the north bank of the Tagus, and before reaching the bridge but having turned round to face west before dropping anchor.

There we stopped there overnight in its calm waters.

I seem to remember being woken by the sound and feel of the main engines being started, so I got up and headed to the restaurant for my breakfast.

As I was eating my English breakfast of bacon, eggs and fried bread, the engines got a bit louder, and we started moving slowly forehead only to suddenly stop with a kind of crunching sound from beneath us. Then a second try and the ship crunched once more and then scraped to a complete halt.

We were well and truly stuck aground and try as the captain might we couldn't move further forward. We were stranded there until the next high tide started coming in.

As soon as we had enough draught, the ship began moving back along the Tagus and out to sea.

Once we left the Tagus and started heading north the captain announced that the stabilisers were to be pulled in so that we could steam faster, as we were running late for the scheduled arrival in Southampton the next morning.

The last games of table tennis were the most unusual as, without the stabilisers, the ship would suddenly lurch to one side or the other more often, and the hit ball would either miss the table completely or hit it earlier than expected. After a while, I gave up and got ready for the last night on board and packed my things ready for departure the next morning.

Being the last night aboard, most of the younger passengers were having a few drinks and enjoying the disco.

Sometime before midnight, we entered the Bay of Biscay where the sea became even more choppy.

I found my partner for the last time and went up to the disco. As we arrived and started to dance, the DJ had just put on the Ballad of John and Yoko which had just got on to, 'Christ, you know it ain't easy, You know how hard it can be, The way things are going, They're going to…' and the arm of the record deck swung violently across the disc while all us dancers were thrown across the dance floor to end up in a pile against the starboard side wall.

At least none of us were crucified but just laughed at the coincidence in the song and pulled each other up to attempt some more dancing, with several repeats of crushes in the next half an hour, by which time we had had enough, and headed off to our bunks below.

My short-term partner and I kissed goodbye, and then I made my way down to my cabin to get ready for sleep.

I woke up as normal and managed to make my way up to the restaurant to have a full breakfast. Then I was back downstairs to get my few things together and ready for disembarkation in plenty of time before docking in Southampton.

I can't remember finding my trunk, but somehow I arrived in customs with both my suitcase and the trunk.

It was then that I lost my keys to both the trunk and the padlock I had put on it.

The female Custom Officer was not pleased.

I asked if there was a pair of cutters that I could use to break the padlock I told her, I had lost the keys to the trunk sometime, so at least the trunk could be opened easily that way.

After some chuntering, she went away and managed to find some cutters to use, and after a quick inspection, I was on my way out where I was greeted by my sister-in-law.

As quickly as I could, I loaded my bag and trunk into her car for the journey to Sevenoaks where her family lived.

Fortunately, they had a quite large house where there was room for me to sleep.

Of course, I had to tell them a little about my experiences but can't remember much more until I travelled to London to the agency where I had been promised a job.

Unsurprisingly, I was greeted with an apology that half the staff had lost their jobs and there was not enough work for more.

I was also told that getting a job despite the portfolio of my work that I assembled and shown to whoever it was who ran the creative team—I can't remember who he was—would be almost impossible, as none of the experienced staff who had been made redundant, had been able to find another job yet.

What to do? I wondered and went out to buy a London paper, where I could find nothing.

Obviously, I would have to find something else, but what? Once more unto the breach my friend!

The rest of my life was perhaps more mundane, but I did have a few odd things happen to me.

The only thing I found and thought would be useful was getting a trainee manager's job with the then Littlewoods Stores. The only odd thing was my first experience of retail, which was to be put into the lingerie section of their store in Chesterfield without being given any prior training.

I had only been on the floor for a couple of minutes when an attractive thirty-year-old, I guessed, woman asked me to measure her bra size. She had to explain the method to me, as there was no staff member near me on the floor to help me.

I remember feeling a bit embarrassed. Perhaps she noticed, judging by the strange smile she gave me, but perhaps she was enjoying this attention from a young man who was using a tape measure to find her breast size and immediately below them to work out the cup size?

I only stayed a few months as, although a useful experience, was not my cup of tea.

Then I saw a chance to work for Mecca to work as a trainee catering manager. Not exactly what I had looked for, but it had its moments.

I started at the Bingo Hall and then moved to their indoor bowling rink, both at Streatham, before receiving the call one Saturday to go immediately to Liverpool ice rink.

At Liverpool ice rink, I became a full catering manager. Not long afterwards there was a bit of a kerfuffle one day when a boy of about seven got a girl to bring a knife into the rink so that he could use it to threaten girls to give him money. He was banned and told to leave and never come back. As a result of this, his two older brothers came to the rink one early evening to threaten staff to allow him back in. They were carrying a steel rod and a piece of four-by-two wood began attacking our door staff with their weapons.

I was in the kitchen at that time and came to the bar in front to see what the noise was about. Fortunately, for me, someone had spilt oil on the floor, and I slipped and fell to the floor as the four-by-two was swung across the top of the bar, just missing my head.

The police soon arrived, and my attacker was caught. A female sergeant had him in front of her to hold on to him as he clumsily fell forward into every pillar he passed as he was taken down the corridor to the outside.

Here he was then thrown head first onto the floor of a police Land Rover, with policemen on either side of him apparently resting their feet on his body.

There was one evening when there was a bit of a disturbance upstairs on the balcony. So I ran up to see what was happening, only to find a couple of youths trying to set light to some loose would outside an unused storage room.

They ran off before I could do anything, but when I looked into the store room, I saw a young couple busily trying to get fully dressed.

It was then that I noticed the storeroom door opposite had been broken into and someone had stolen some spirits and then left through the window onto the roof.

When I looked out, I could just see two figures disappearing over the roof at the back.

I made sure that the room was locked as securely as I could then called the police. For the rest of the evening, I continued as if nothing had happened until the rink closed.

Then a colleague asked if he could give me a lift to my car. We turned the corner into a road behind the rink. "My car was over there. It's gone!" I gasped. Mr Kaye, who believed the Beatles had used his name in one of their songs, quickly turned and took me to the police station.

These two policemen who had just arrived behind the desk, where I was explaining what had happened, looked at me and said, "We want to speak to you." Then they asked me to follow them to a small room.

They were just asking me where I was at ten o'clock.

"I was with him," I said pointing at another officer who was just passing the door.

After a short discussion with him, the two officers explained that my car had hit a few others when being chased, and the driver had run off. My car was a right-off, it also had a few bottles of whisky and others in the back, probably stolen from the rink that night. I had to buy a new car after this.

On another late afternoon, when we were closed, I needed to talk to the manager, and when I opened his door, I discovered him standing over our cashier, her head between his legs and her skirt bottom high on her back completely exposing her knickered bottom that Bert Sale was smacking as he bent over her.

"What on earth are you doing?" I asked as he let the girl go, and she dashed out of the office. "If I catch you again," I continued. "I'll contact your wife."

I didn't know what else I should do in those days.

A couple of days later I unexpectedly got a call to go back up to London to work in a very popular disco again in Streatham.

One night at the Bali Hai disco, our bouncers, who we thought were on the fiddle, unexpectedly gave me a glass of Coke. An action which had never happened before—it was laced with LSD, as they were expecting me to check on their fiddle at the door so had it prepared for me.

I quickly realised what they had done and went to the office to sit down and call for help from the nearby dance hall. While sitting, I found myself somehow inside the patterned wallpaper, then I thought I would put my ice skates on and jump through plate glass windows onto the ice rink below.

Fortunately, our cashier stopped me just as I was about to start my run towards the glass.

The police had been called and asked that I be taken to hospital to get a blood sample.

I went in a taxi with our cashier, with cars coming towards us and seemingly coming right through our car as we drove.

When we arrived at the hospital, a doctor wearing enormous pebble glasses took many goes in each arm before getting a sample. It took a couple of days to get over it all, particularly those eyes that seemed to come right into my head.

Things went on much as usual for a while until later on I was asked to work at another Mecca disco down in Guildford. My job included having to cook meals there when our chef ran out for no apparent reason. One of our customers that night was Engelbert Humperdinck who asked for a steak.

Unfortunately, I dropped it on the floor when getting it out of the grill. Apparently, he was in a hurry to get it, so I picked it up and put it straight on his plate. He ate the lot with no complaint!

Shortly after this, I returned to the Bali Hai where things were much as before. Friday and Saturday nights always being crowded, and I sometimes had to go downstairs and out of the emergency exit and back in through the front door to get from one end of the bar to the other.

We were closed on Mondays and Tuesdays, so these were our 'weekends off'.

There was only one exception to this when one Tuesday I was asked to greet and show the place off to the Miss World competitors before the competition took place.

I was surprised that I did not fancy any of them. Without make-up, they looked like anyone on the street but perhaps more attractive than most.

However, it was at the Bali H'ai where I met my future wife.

Otherwise, the busy nights would include being visited by the Clapham Junction Mob and, standing at one end of the bar, detectives from the Metropolitan police chatting away with senior members of the criminal community, or so I was informed.

I can't remember which New Year's Eve it was, but quite out of the blue, I was offered and received an escort for part of my drive home to Staplehurst.

I was no sooner in my car when a car with blue lights flashing arrived and signalled me to follow. Halfway across London, another car took over until I was on the road to Bromley.

Later that year the manager was on holiday and there was a shortage of bouncers, so I was on the door with two new ones.

We had a fairly close relationship with the local police station, and I had previously warned them about possible trouble over the weekend when I took a couple of cases of lager for them on Tuesday. On Friday, I don't know where it came from, but there was a further warning that there might be trouble when the police shifts were changing that Saturday, so again I went to the station and asked for some presence immediately the new shift was to come on.

There were police detectives in the club and patrols during the evening outside.

At precisely 11:00 pm, there was a sudden push in the crowd.

I was in front of the only two bouncers I could get when, out of the blue a couple of punches hit me below my eyes, cutting my skin in both places.

One of the bouncers turned and ran upstairs leaving me on the floor and the other bouncer tried to hold off the crush, just as the police swarmed into the crowd.

They managed to arrest the man who had hit me with his diamond ring.

I don't know how it happened, but a manager from one of the other two establishments in Streatham arrived to help out, while I was taken to the hospital for four or five stitches to be put in under each eye.

Despite the change to my features a new member of staff seemed attracted to me and I, her and very soon we became close and finally married.

I had seen false eyelashes worn by ladies for the eyelid but didn't expect to have the NHS supply me with some semi-permanent ones on the lower one.

The incident had a bad effect on me despite a little donation for my troubles, and I started looking for other work but gave up after not finding anything interesting.

So not very long after this again I moved, this time back to Staplehurst and got a temporary job at Bachelors Foods, where I produced the very first batch of Cuppa Soup. Another claim to fame!

A couple of months after this I became assistant manager of Charing Cross Hospital Staff Club.

This allowed me to return to London and live in a flat in Hammersmith owned by the hospital, so my wife and I could live together.

The then manager did not have a commercial side to him and turnover was just about holding its own, so he was let go and I took charge.

This allowed me to increase turnover nearly tenfold over four years by hiring out our hall to the likes of the BBC for rehearsals like Angels and a couple of live Nationwide programmes.

A couple of times I was asked by one of the TV crew if I would like to be taken around Television Centre.

During one such visit, I was just allowed to wander and decide to take the next door on the left, opened it and walked to a studio only to find myself inside the Tardis, and when I stopped in front of a green screen, I looked up at a monitor to see myself being sent spinning far away into the Universe.

One of my cleaning staff rushed in one morning, his face was white. He made some noises in Spanish I didn't understand but asked him to sit down and explain the situation.

"My wife's had triplets," he gushed.

Obviously, this was unexpected, so I told him to take the rest of the week off and assured him he would still get paid. This was not normal then.

I would always listen to any problems with cleaning and other staff and encouraged them to tell me how things could be improved and why. Even if the resolution was costly, I could see how an operation would be simpler and produce a better finish and follow their ideas. Praise and appreciate anyone's ideas, even if I had to turn the odd one down, they always appreciated being listened to and were excellent employees.

One of the celebrities I met at the staff club was Lena Zavaroni, who had her own show then and did the rehearsals at the club each week.

One day she came up to me, almost as though she was a naughty little girl, and asked if it would be alright if she could use our swimming pool. Of course, I said yes, and she gave me a nice broad smile.

One Saturday night I was talking to the organiser of a group regularly using our hall when he asked me to turn around and shake hands with a guest. When I did there was a man dressed in a white suit, with two armed men behind him. I dutifully shook his hand and after he moved off I turned back to the organiser.

He told me that if I was in his country and the visitor did not like my handshake, he would have it cut off.

I was later told that the man was Saddam Hossein.

At much the same time, I developed a friendship with Chris Spedding, a guitarist and singer who was also Uncle Bulgaria of the Wombles.

He lived near where we were then living with our first son. Usually, I went to his little flat, but once or twice he visited me before he decided to go off to America. Just before he went on his tour, I made one last visit to his basement flat.

Instead of his usual welcoming grin, he looked as though he had been kicked in the teeth.

No wonder! "Earlier in the day," he told me, "a close friend of mine took a song I had written and got it published under his name."

I just did not know how to console him, nor whether to ask the thief's name, so I asked him what he would do now.

It was then that he said he was going to tour the U.S. among some other things he planned to do.

At least he had some definite plans, I thought, as I wished him well and said goodbye for the very last time.

Then my wife and I moved to a maisonette in Harrow.

Soon after this, my son managed to climb a unit and reached out to pull a hot teapot of water over his head and had to be taken to a specialist burns hospital.

I left work as soon as I could to see him. I can still remember walking into his cubicle when he was in his mum's arms, and he put his arms out towards me, tears streaming from slits in his now swollen eyelids.

Not long after this, we journeyed north to live in Newcastle, where I managed to gain a Diploma in Management Studies. One day walking into town and passing three double-decker buses that were stuck in the snow that had fallen overnight to the height of a bonnet of a car.

I did a couple of jobs in a short time living there before moving to manage Washington Arts Centre. There I increased a once-a-month Art Mart that began with twenty stalls to more than ninety twice monthly that increased revenue from this source alone from twelve hundred pounds a year to more than eleven thousand.

A little a year later, Rev Shegog asked me if I might like to run and develop a completely new idea: Action Retirement Centre in Sunderland. This operated five days a week and provided a daily range of activities for the over-fifties, as well as a trained support group helping people, who were over-dependent on prescription drugs, to reduce or stop their addiction.

It became quite well known, and I had the pleasure of a reporter and cameraman, Don McCullin from The Times Sunday Supplement, coming to see what this novel enterprise was all about. Apparently, it was worth three full pages. I was also interviewed by both the local press and Radio Four and spoke at a meeting at Sheffield University.

Teaching and lecturing were my further activities after gaining a DMS and later, when we moved to Sunderland, a B.Ed.

While doing the course at Sunderland I was in charge of security and safety during evening events in the Students Union.

At the start of the second year, I organised a first aid session where we learnt how to do resuscitation. This was fortunate because, the next week, I was walking into the town centre when I saw a man fall off his ladder as he was stepping off the roof of a house.

He fell onto the flagstone-covered frontage, and I rushed to help him and found he was not breathing. I was quickly joined by a passing nurse and together we carried out resuscitation until the ambulance arrived.

Later I heard that he had survived.

I took up a post at Consett College where a quite different event occurred that has stayed with me ever since.

It happened at the start of the last class on Friday.

When everyone was settling down in their seats, a female student approached and asked to talk to me. I could see in her eyes and face something like had I felt after measuring up the explosion in South Africa.

So I told the rest of the class to go to the library and do homework if they wanted but not to cause a fuss.

I asked her if she would rather see our permanent personal counsellor or a female teacher, as I guessed what she wanted to talk about was very personal, but she said, "No, I'd rather speak to you."

I pulled up chairs so that she could sit near me but not in such a position that anyone looking in might think something else was going on.

Firstly, she told me about being locked in a cupboard every time her dad thought she had not acted properly as she was told. He and her mum divorced and social services intervened. Then, a few years later, her mum took another partner. I cannot describe the intimate details when she told me about what he did to her when he was 'putting her to bed at night'.

Once again, social services were involved, and she spent a difficult time with another family. Eventually, after many requests, she was allowed to live with her grandparents.

Suffice it to say that I was so moved by her story that I hardly slept during the weekend, but I was sworn to secrecy, so I felt I couldn't talk to anyone again and just had to soak it all up by myself.

A bit later I felt very honoured to have been chosen to listen to her story—it is always nice to know that you can be trusted for such as this had been.

About six years later I received a letter from her in Canada to say that she was now happily married and had just had a baby boy.

A bit before this time, my wife and I divorced, but I had both boys stay with me on alternate weekends until they finished school. I took them to the Lake District to climb the hills or do some rock climbing on Dartmoor during a holiday in the region. They were a bit adventurous like me.

Like most things in my life, there has been a lot to learn and put into practice when I have needed to.

I may not have grown rich in money terms, but I have had a lot of pleasure and satisfaction from what I did. Particularly with students and by employing people whose applications would normally have been discarded but proved to have very good skills with just a little advice and training. Everyone was lovely to work with.

Another thing that pleased me as a lecturer was developing a course for adult students who wanted to gain qualifications in management when I worked at Derwentside College.

One in leadership was fairly straightforward but that for management at degree level was much more difficult, particularly for people who had low or no formal qualifications.

The normal approach was standard lectures in a classroom followed by some kind of examination. This was often difficult when it came to subjects like financial management and/or candidates with poor writing skills.

If their senior management was supportive a quiet approach was very effective.

Mine was to make all assessments based on problem-solving assignments relating to their own workplaces and the covered topics we covered in class.

When it came to understanding or producing balance sheets and profit and loss accounts, the methodology and probable consequences of reality or potential changes became much more understandable. The only issue was the need for me to approve what they intended to do before they set off to do each one.

Of course, that involved my visiting their workplaces in order to understand the business and see for myself what they could do to fit with the standards required.

This included my being willing to receive calls at home from students seeking advice, occasionally at midnight on a Sunday. Sometimes the call was to request a further visit as a description over the phone was not enough.

There was one particular student who had left school at fifteen with no qualifications to become a butcher's boy who I shall never forget.

When he was in his late thirties he changed to work on the production line of an international paint manufacturer. The hierarchy allowed him to use the secretary to type up what he dictated to her.

When he had achieved all externally assessed satisfactory assignments, he was soon promoted to production manager.

In a short time, he reduced the level of stock held by the company, while increasing the range of products sold and staff required as well as reducing the delay time for deliveries to be made.

A colleague, who also passed, became personnel manager.

The investment by the company was obviously worth it.

I also spent some time teaching in a secondary school and once I was asked to help when some pupils were being taken to London to look around. I was given time off one evening and went to the House of Commons to watch a debate.

I sat in the middle of the public gallery and two people came to sit beside me, though there was plenty of space elsewhere. To my surprise, they were Esther Rantzen and Michael Palin.

After I retired from teaching, I took on a part-time job again working for Ipsos Mori—this time the London version.

I quite enjoyed travelling around parts of the Northeast to do the interviewing until an event near Hexham.

I had a number of properties to visit in and around a village. There was one that I had to go to that had a long drive. Normal practice was to find parking close to the entrance, but the road was narrow and there was nowhere I could see to park, so I drove up the drive and parked beside the far side of a mansion.

I had just gotten out of my car with my gear and turned the corner of the building when a man confronted me shouting to get off his land otherwise I might be shot.

He did not let me tell him who I was and what I was doing but continued to harangue me until I got back into my car.

Gingerly, I reversed it, so he would not shout at me for going on his grass. Then I drove slowly forward past his house so as not to upset him again.

As I passed a flight of stone steps, out he came again shouting and pointing a shotgun at me. Several times he shouted, "Get off my land and don't come back again or you might be shot."

The gun was pointed at my head, so I drove as fast as I could to get away.

When I was far enough away, I stopped to wait for my shaking to end.

After a while, I drove off and stopped by an open pub to find out where to find a police station.

There I reported what had happened, and still a bit shaky, I drove slowly home.

That night I dreamed of going back to his house in the dark and slitting my throat to die bleeding on his front steps.

This thought was only increased when a police officer from Hexham called to tell me that the man had been visited in the early hours when he denied everything I had reported.

I don't recall quite how it happened but, not long after the call, an ambulance came to take me to the hospital where I stayed for a couple of weeks suffering from PTSD.

The treatment continued for some months before I was my old self again.

Looking back on my life at work and elsewhere, it probably would not have been so enjoyable and generally effective if, when I was young I was not given a lot of freedom to explore. I was also encouraged to play team games and activities like playing draughts, chess and Shove ha'penny with my dad as well as later playing the likes of whist and bridge, which involved a degree of problem-solving.

Certainly, I had to use that ability, when I took Teachers' Pensions and the Pensions Ombudsman to appeal in the Rolls Building in London, when I had to take on two barristers supported by solicitors to win my case as a litigant in person.

When I won it altered the way the law was interpreted.

Fortunately, I had the support of my sons in court, as it gave me more confidence.

Being part of the school cadets and going with my dad to see how he managed also played their part, as I developed organising skills that I needed to argue my case cogently.

Furthermore, adventures in South Africa, including breaking Apartheid rules sometimes, had a bearing on the way I later treated staff and students.

I am still in contact with some through the Internet.

So I consider I have had a generally very happy life and feel rewarded for what I have done, and despite the divorce, I am delighted to see how well my children have fared. Now I also have four grandchildren and am married again, this time to a lady whose advertisement I saw in a local newspaper, that purported to say that she lived in North Yorkshire.

I soon found out that she and her daughter actually lived in Donetsk. So after a number of contacts through the Internet and a few telephone calls, I went to Ukraine to find out what she was like in the flesh.

Obviously, something else also worked out, and we still live happily together!

The main thing that I see is that it is important to believe in yourself if you want to achieve anything, however big or small. It also helps if you have the support of your family or people you respect behind you.

If you employ others, much the same is true, but you must show that you trust them first.